Being a Man in a Woman's World

World

Start having the relationships you deserve

Dennis W. Neder, DM

Being a Man in a Woman's World

Revision 1.0

Cover design by Joseph E. Duggan, Inc. JEDI, Pasadena, CA

Publisher: Remington Publications
                P.O. Box 10702
                Glendale, CA 91209-3702
                818-246-2058
                www.remingtonpublications.com

ISBN 0-9701713-0-7

Printed in the United States

To my mother, Lois who taught me that life is about smiles and laughter – both those you give and those you get.

To my father, Joseph who made me understand that one's word is all you have – and all you need.

A special thanks goes to my friends and reviewers who, through their unique insight, understanding and wisdom, this book meets and serves its market.

Finally, to those women that have shown me the way through their tenderness, caring, love, and especially, their commitment to my understanding of their souls. I have, and continue to learn. I love you.

Table of Contents

Preface

Why did I write this book?

I once thought there'd be many books like this one. After doing some research, I found that there were very few, and none of them really provided the type of material in this book. They talk about how to communicate with a woman (a good thing), how to make love to a woman (a good thing), and how to win the woman of your dreams (a very, very bad thing). From this point on, whether you believe it or not, you are *the* winner in the world of dating. I'm going to tell you how the woman of your dreams is going to win *you* (with your help, of course).

Through my experience in business, sales and marketing, and my experience in the dating world, I have learned that there are just a few rules that make up any successful venture. Whether it's selling websites, clothing, insurance, or yourself, the rules are the same. This is a great realization for any man because it takes this mysterious process of meeting and dating women and reduces it to a small number of simple steps. And, these steps work.

You are going to get the tools that many of the world's most successful salespeople take years to learn, make some real, concrete decisions about your goals, create a plan, put it into action, review and adjust it, and follow up on it, through the steps in this book. You will also get keys to actually communicating with these women (a necessary skill). Finally, as you succeed, you will get the tools to handle the many problems that can come from the dating experience.

I encourage you to pass this information along. Not very many of our fathers felt we needed to have the knowledge in this book (in fact, few of them learned it!). But, to gain control and get the things we want in our relationships with women, we have to perfect our skills. Once these are tested and proved, we have to begin sharing them with others. This is good for men but it is also good for women because they will get what they want too.

Have you been less than satisfied with your dating life? Have the women you've met been lacking in one or more ways? Do you feel unfulfilled? Are you having trouble finding, meeting, attracting, or keeping a woman? Isn't it about time that you found the problems and corrected them? In fact, isn't it about time that all men got themselves together and corrected many of the problems that seem to propagate from generation to generation?

Almost every man seems to have the same problems with women. We even joke about these problems as though we're just never going to understand women and therefore it's all right. It's time to finally get these things corrected.

This book is written for that reason – to help you get your dating problems and your problems with women corrected – and to help you enjoy your relationships in a new and unique way. May you find new power and joy in being a man. I wish this for you.

Introduction

If you're easily offended, please put this book down. If you're in a happy, committed, monogamous relationship, put this book down. If you are happy with your present level of success with women, put this book down. If you believe that you were meant to be manipulated, abused, ignored, or in any other way mistreated by women, put this book down. If you are a woman, please, put this book down!

If, on the other hand you want to learn how to have better, more fulfilling relationships with women; you want to be better liked by, experience deeper love with, and be completely appreciated and respected by women, then read on – you've just found your answer!

This will be an important century for men and women. We are in a battle – a fight for happiness and fulfillment. Just like every other war, we have two opposing sides, weapons, winners and losers, and a battlefield. Who are the opponents? You are on one side, and every woman you have ever known or will ever know is on the other. The weapons? This book is one of the few weapons available for men. Some others include advice from your friends and family, some radio talk shows, a few late night television programs and some magazine articles. Women on the other hand have many. In fact they spend their lives collecting the weapons with which they will meet you on the field of battle. Where is this battlefield? Every bar, personal ad, telephone call, office, store, health club, organization, and even your friends' houses.

Please keep in mind as you read this book, I am not talking about the "battle of the sexes" here, nor anything else so trite. I am talking about your own very personal battle, your own personal war, to win in the interactions you face every day in dealing with the opposite sex – and to enjoy the spoils of your victory.

Why did I feel compelled to write this book? Because every day, men are confronted with the same issues, the same challenges as our fathers and our grandfathers. You see, while you and your buddies were playing "army," building tree houses, and blowing up toy models, your battlefield opponent was learning the art and skills of this war. Even now, she and her girlfriends are constantly practicing and perfecting their techniques. In fact, as you will soon see, our families, our government, our society, and we ourselves are all trying to help them win! Help them to **beat us**!

And, what is the result of all of this fighting? Men die younger. Men spend most all of their lives in jobs they hate, in relationships that are unfulfilling and unhealthy at least, and in fear. Our options in life are extremely limited at best. We are given little choice other than to go to work and strive to succeed or become a bum. I am using the term "succeed" to mean, "earn bucks." Do you find this to be a limited definition? Is this offensive to you? I hope so! If not, then you have bought into popular thought promoted by those that want you to lose your war.

As we will see, we men are sold on many of these lies. Worse yet, many of us actually believe them or even help sell them to other men! "Popular" thought doesn't mean "correct" thought. If you disbelieve this, try following the majority of investors in the stock market. Only small percentages ever make any real money. They don't do this by following the majority's direction.

My friend, get your armor on and turn the page. You are preparing for the war of your life, and for your life itself.

What This Book Is

In a nutshell, this book is a culmination of relationship skills, business acumen, marketing expertise, interpersonal and managerial skills, observation, research, education and understanding. By taking the best of all of these things and combining them into a model that works over and over again in almost every other aspect of a person's life, you can achieve any level of success you desire in the world of relationships.

Are you a salesman?

Have you ever sold anything? Have you ever held a job? Have you ever had a relationship with a woman? Have you ever been married? Have you ever talked your parents into lending you the car? Have you ever gotten your sister or brother to do part of your chores for you? If you've answered "yes" to any of these questions, then some selling has been done somewhere.

I can't tell you how many times I have been told, "I can't (or don't want to) sell." What these people are saying is, "I can't convince people." The error here is in thinking that sales means convincing someone of something.

The real key to selling is this: Find the person who wants to buy what you have to sell and make it worth their while to buy what you are selling.

This book is about helping you to find the women who want to buy what you have to sell, delivering the pitch, and then closing the sale.

Because I have worked with so many people in my career, I can tell you that first, everybody thinks that they or their business is unique, and second that nobody is that unique. Almost every technique that works well in one industry, or with one type of person will work with other industries and with other types of people. This is an exciting concept – go back and re-read this paragraph.

Too many are the times that I've heard someone say that they are different from everyone else and that's why they can't meet women. My friend, as special as you are, you are not *so* special as to fail every single time! The real key is to get back up to bat. Never give up. Believe me, you can do it!

Many moons ago, I had the great fortune to study hypnotherapy. Much of my general understanding of how people think and react initially came from that study. I then began a search for greater understanding of people using the experiences of others as a guide. I further refined this understanding by reading and testing my knowledge. Where it failed, I adjusted it and tried it again until I found success.

Through my own businesses, I have had the perfect learning environment for human interactions. Dealing with clients, vendors, and employees has helped hone my understanding of people and their motivations. Working with others in their own studies on psychology, sales, and business has also greatly added to my understanding.

My own dating life is also a cornerstone of this book. I have dated many women from many different backgrounds and cultures. Each one has helped to educate me – partly because I asked, partly because I listened (and then listened some more), and partly because I screwed up. Where I screwed up, they tried to help "educate" me – and I love them all for it. Eventually, after enough repeating of the same lessons over and over again, I was promoted to higher levels – and finally, better relationships.

Much reading, trial and error, testing and correcting was the birth of this book. I have asked my friends and lovers about their experiences and beliefs, and why they do things in certain ways. When they gave me the answers, I questioned the answers. When they answered that, I asked them why they answered as they did. The education you can get if you just ask is amazing!

Keep in mind as you read this book that not every woman you meet will fit everything said here exactly. For this reason I don't use terms like "everybody" or "all women" when discussing people's behavior. However, if you use this book as a guide, you will find that so much of it applies consistently to so many women that you will apply its message easily.

My friends (male and female) have discussed everything you will find here in the book. The things that will make you more powerful are here – a compendium of information, edited and audited for you to digest. And, it is a celebration of what makes us men.

What This Book Is Not

This book is absolutely not a manual on how to get a woman to do your bidding. Although, if you follow the steps outlined herein, she will *want* to please you. "You can't push a chain uphill," as the saying goes. Likewise, you can't convince anyone to do anything for you that they wouldn't otherwise want to do. You can however make it worthwhile for women to respond in more appropriate, predictable ways.

This book is also not a sex manual. There are plenty of good texts on sexual technique that you should have already read or plan to read. On the other hand, some basic clues will be provided to help you to get the kind of sexual partner you deserve. Good sexual technique doesn't come naturally to men or women. People understand their own needs, but usually not the needs of the opposite sex. Your sexual prowess is not based on what you think, but what your partner thinks. You'll have to make a commitment to becoming a "sex-pert." After all, you want success and satisfaction in your sex life, right? To get it in the abundance you deserve, you'll have to learn to give it as well.

I also didn't write this book to trash women. I **love** women! They are wonderful, interesting creatures with more facets than a diamond. On the other hand, they have been trained from birth to manipulate *you* into doing their bidding. This is portrayed as something cute in every aspect of society. That is what makes it particularly insidious – the fact that this type of manipulation is going on every day. Think about this. How would your male friends view you if you tried to pull some of the same things that you let women pull? You'd be laughed at! In fact, we as men know that these maneuvers are going on, but we continue to fall for them over and over again – because they work! And, they work every time to our detriment. Let this madness stop!

This book is not an apology for anything. If you're looking for some good old-fashioned guilt, look elsewhere. I don't want you to have to apologize for being a man ever again. Every member of this modern society needs to understand that men are highly evolved creatures and have solid patterns, reasons and capabilities necessary to ensure the success of the society. We are not just sperm donors with wallets!

This is also not some new-aged rhetoric on your inner child, banging some friggin' drum, or getting in touch with your feminine side. Don't expect to be coddled or nurtured by this book. It is a kick in the pants to get moving; to collect what is yours; to retrieve your testicles and put them back where they belong; and to enjoy the benefits of taking responsibility for your life and your love.

It is time to stop the nonsense and to stop playing the victim. You are the only one responsible for you – in every way. Stop trying to find someone else that will make you rich, handsome and powerful. Stop trying to find someone that will lead you to the love of your life. When good things happen, recognize that it is because of you. When bad things happen – you again! Stop trying to find a scapegoat, or someone else that is to blame. It is you, you, **you**!

Finally, this book is not for women, but women will benefit from its content! Many women will read this book and huff that it's just more garbage from men. But, don't be fooled – many women feel threatened by this type of information. If *you* are in control (like you should be), then what is left for them? We've reached a time in history when dissatisfaction with relationships is at an all-time high. The women have had their shot at it for the last century. It's time for men to take control and make it work. Sorry ladies, but don't be scared; we're going to give you what you want – finally. And, you're going to give us what we want – finally. It's time for us all to win!

Notes to Women

So, you didn't heed my warning in the introduction to put this book down, eh? Not surprising.

Men: please note that women are trying every day to find out what you think. Women will read this book in an attempt to gain even greater influence over **you**! They are looking for new tools for **their** weapons chest, new ways of getting you to do what they want. Every time I mentioned to a woman that I was writing this book I received the same response; "Ohhh, I want to read it!" Men, they want to read it to know what you're thinking.

Women: Is it a bad thing that you want to know more about the way men think? No, of course not. (In fact, I secretly salute you!) The problem is that most of your information heretofore has come from **other women**! You read magazines that specifically target you with promises to "Understand what he really means when he says..." and "Know when he really is in love with you..." and so on. I sometimes wonder if these women have ever even talked with a man regarding the issues they write about. (Yes, men, I know you feel the same way.)

If you have chosen to read this book to gain a greater insight into men's thinking, I believe that you will find it valuable. If you are hoping to find some fault in my logic, only hoping to point out where I'm wrong – forget it. Simply wishing a thing won't make it so. I intend to present a man's view of a man's world. If you don't like it, there are a thousand other sources that will give you exactly what *you* want, but probably no better an understanding than you already think you have. Thus, don't bother sending me hate mail – I'll probably just find it funny.

We live in a time where so many people are espousing the popular view and giving "feel-good" advice rather than looking at the facts and working from there. You may not like what you are going to read, but I'll bet you'll like the outcome. Why would I make this bet? Because I have talked to many women who are looking for their men to be men. Not the media's view of men, and not the view proposed by so many self-help books, women's articles, and talk shows. I'm talking about the man who is confident and self-assured. A man who is going somewhere and wants the perfect partner to complement himself, and wants to complement someone else. A man that cares enough to let (and encourage) you to be *your* best.

By now you've no doubt read that most men are confused by what women say they want. To quote, "they want a man to be strong, but sensitive," "they want a man to be caring and considerate of their feelings," or "they want a man to really listen to them."

All of this may or may not be true. In fact, it is all both true and false. The problem with these types of statements is that first they are based on many assumptions. Assumptions about the people involved. Assumptions about the type of relationships between the people, and assumptions about the intended audience. Second, they don't take into account what the men really want. Third, they are typically made by researchers and authors that simply parrot popular culture rather than seeking a better understanding of both the meaning of the statements and the eventual implications of them.

Women, make no mistake about it; men want to give you what you want. They also want to get what they need in return. This isn't so hard to accept, is it? The real problem here is *how* to go about it. The last millennium has promoted the idea that women can cleverly manipulate their men into being the person of their dreams. Look at writings, plays, and music from these decades. Look at popular television shows and books from just the past 50 years.

Unfortunately, all too often, society accepts with humor some women's positions such as interest in men for what they can provide. Sure, they want the love and caring and all the other good things that go along with it. But as the old saying goes, "it's just as easy to fall in love with a rich man as a poor one." This is offensive! It imposes the same stereotypes that we are trying to correct – men as sperm donors and wallets.

Wouldn't it be better for your man be the strong, capable partner that you know he can be? He can provide you a lifetime of security and comfort and even revel in you for being the woman of *his* dreams. For you, this is all I ask.

The Test

If you've ever been in a relationship with a woman that's lasted more than a few weeks, you've experienced it. If not, be forewarned – you will experience it and it's not going to be pretty. It's that little quirky situation where the woman does something totally outside of normal – totally unexpected, and totally ridiculous, all for no apparent reason. This is what I call "the test."

What Specifically is "The Test"?

It can take an unlimited number of forms – from not being ready to go out on your date, to "forgetting" to call you when you both agreed, to pulling something so egregious that you are ready to explode. There are far too many different types of tests that you will face to describe all of them here. However, be assured that you will be tested.

How you handle your test will be the defining factor in how your relationship (or lack of one) will progress. Make no mistake about it; you have one chance and one chance only to succeed at the test. Should you fail, you are likely to be in for more trouble than you bargained for.

Here is an example of a test that I faced. I once had a date with a woman I will call Sarah. We had met only a few weeks before and this was the second time we'd been together. She was a classical musician and had a very classic style of dress and mannerism.

Sarah and I were going to a classical recital on this date and then dinner. This was all very artsy and upper class, so I dressed in a nice turtleneck sweater, slacks and jacket. When I arrived to pick up Sarah (on time), she answered the door in an old sweatshirt and jeans. She was very up and happy to see me and bounced in to get her purse so we could run out the door.

Now, I had two choices – either blow off the way she was dressed and just go and try to hide my embarrassment, or take action. I chose the latter. I grabbed her by the hand, and pulled her back into her apartment. We marched right into her bedroom where I opened the closet. She stood behind me dumbfounded as I went through her clothes and picked out a lovely black dress and a pair of matching heels. I laid the dress on her bed and on the way out said, "That will look lovely with some pearls or simple gold jewelry" as I closed the door for her to dress. She was ready in less than five minutes (record time for any woman!).

Now, what do you think her attitude was upon her return? If you said irritated, you lose a point. If you said angry, you lose two points. If you said compliant, you win 10 points!

When she emerged, she had her hair done, and even updated her makeup to suit the new attire. She came out and actually modeled for me and waited for my approval, which came after a short appreciation of the beauty she created for me. When we returned home that night, we engaged in some really serious sex. More important, I never had to pass any more tests.

Men, if you've left your testicles on some woman's nightstand, it's time to go retrieve them.

This is an important lesson. It took me many years, but I finally figured it out. In fact, the women I dated were so patient with me, they just kept on giving me more and more tests, until I finally wised up! All right, maybe I'm not that smart, but there is no reason why you should have to suffer the same humiliation and anxiety that I faced. I am going to give you the tools to pass your tests on the first try – every time.

You see, women truly want to believe that they are spending their time with someone of substance, someone who knows what they want and will make things that way – even if they have to risk or expose themselves. This is the first rule of the test – deciding that you are in control in the relationship. This means that you absolutely cannot let your woman walk all over you, at any time. Why not? Because you can't predict when the test will occur. Thus, you have to decide up front to handle every battle as a potential test.

What would I have done if Sarah had gotten huffy and insulted, and refused to go? I would have calmly, and without anger, told her, "Okay, when you're over this little tantrum, call me – but not one minute before!" Then, I would have turned and walked out the door, called my "backup" woman, and gone to the concert. We'll talk about the "backup" later under "The Plan."

Further, I would have forgotten about Sarah the instant I walked out her door. This is for three reasons – first, if she had really been upset about my reaction, she would be telling me that she was looking for a man to dump on. Frankly, I don't have the time or interest in being this person. I'll let some other poor sap fill that spot. Second, there are so many other women out there, and third, I don't fall in love until *after* I own the goods.

I have had other situations where I did exactly this – walked out and put the ball squarely back in the woman's lap to "shape up." What happened? If they were looking for someone of substance, they always called because there aren't that many of us out there (yet!). By walking out without any anger or remorse, I am saying that I'm important enough to me, to be treated properly. How about you? You're important enough too and deserve to be taken care of and respected by a woman. You just have to tell her so.

Why Do We Get The Test?

I spent many years pondering this question. Until I had a better understanding of what women were looking for in men, it always left me confused. Think about this – would you purposefully do something that would make a woman angry or make her think you're an idiot? Of course not! But, women do this. So, why do they do it?

The first answer is simple – women want to be involved with men that can pass their tests. You had better get that fact firmly embedded into your mind. If you can't pass their tests, you're never going to have the type of relationship you want to have with women. This doesn't mean that women won't date you – they will. And, they'll continue to try to abuse you, manipulate you, or change you from the person they fell in love with to their imaginary "ideal man." How many times have you seen women that go after assholes and try to make them gentlemen? Then, when they find out that they can't, they'll claim that the man is the problem! Women have a romantic belief in what their men should be. The knight in shining armor isn't far from reality, but there are so many other things that women also want. By passing the test, you're saying that you are that man. However, it isn't enough to just pass a test; you're going to have to vanquish it! We'll see how to do this shortly.

After giving you many tests, if you still aren't the man she imagines you should be, she'll fall out of love with you – treating you as though (and telling everyone within earshot that) you lied to her! In fact, many men feel guilty as though they have done something wrong! How can you be her perfect ideal man? Simple – just pass her test. That's all it takes.

Why, specifically, do we get tests? Here are the reasons:

- Women learn to test you from an early age.
  It is part of their relationship training. Again, even popular culture promotes the test. Examples of tests are all around us in movies, books, and television. It is often used as a source of humor. In fact, the men portrayed almost always fail the tests. The next time you see some man running around in a movie, doing something stupid because of a woman, you're probably seeing "The Test" right before your eyes. Watch what is happening closely– he is making a

fool of himself to try to impress the woman. How cute. That, my friend, is how society views the test, and *you*, if you don't do something about it.

- Women spend a lot of time dreaming of men that can pass their tests.
  Along with dreaming about their marriages, women dream of test-passing men. These men are even immortalized in women's literature and fantasy. They want you to be that man (and, so do you).

- Women are more discriminating about their partners than men.
  Women have a subconscious need to be with men that can protect and provide. You prove your ability to do this by passing their tests.

- People expect women to test their men.
  Our culture doesn't impose the stigma of being direct, open and forthright on women as they do on men. Women have an innate understanding of this and impose this testing process on each other as part of their relationship training. They expect men to jump through hoops for them. In fact, they'll even discuss your success or failure!

Whether you like it or not, women will spend time talking about you and your reactions to their tests. Here's a story that illustrates this point:

A number of years ago, I began casually dating a woman I'll call Catherine. One day after about a month or so, we came back from dinner to find a bouquet of flowers on her doorstep, with a note from some other man she was seeing. I didn't have a problem with this, as she and I were not in an exclusive relationship. She was worried about how I would react, but I just ignored it.

We were sitting in her living room enjoying some wine while she tried to explain away the flowers when the doorbell rang. She said, "Quick – hide!" Huh? Hide?? I've never hidden from anyone. She said, "Hurry – it's him!" I assumed that "him" meant the person that sent the flowers. So, angrily, I followed her into the kitchen, away from the window. She was very nervous as the guy kept ringing the doorbell. After a few minutes of this madness, I told her that if she wasn't going to answer the door, I would. She pleaded with me not to, but finally agreed to go talk to him.

She answered the door and then stepped outside to speak to him. I waited about 10 minutes while they talked and finally I had had enough. I went to the door and opened it. They both spun around with surprise and just stared at me. I put my hand out to the guy and introduced myself, saying that I was "the guy you didn't know about." It was obvious from everybody's reactions that she was playing this man, and that he knew nothing of me. I said, "I'm not going to hang around here while you two work out your problems. Catherine, don't call me until they *are* worked out – understand?" She nodded affirmatively and I left. Within an hour I got a phone call from her saying that she had dumped the guy. So, I asked her for his telephone number. Reluctantly, she gave it to me and I confirmed that she had indeed dumped him.

Now, within a week, I was the man her girlfriends *had* to meet. They kept saying, "Oh, yeah – I've heard about *you*!" In fact, a number of them actually asked me out (I had to decline of course), because I had passed their tests too! The point of this story is that women are going to talk about your success or failure. Commit right now to being the man that they'll have to meet – the "success."

How to Spot The Test

It helps to recognize that you're being tested when it happens. However, tests can be so subtle or even masked as other things, that we often miss them. Thus, it is more important to establish a foundation for handling all situations – including tests – up front. You do this by making three simple decisions – you decide that you will not, under any circumstances:

- Relinquish control of the relationship,
- Be mistreated or treated with disrespect, or,
- Deal with pure craziness. No exceptions.

You must adopt these rules if you want confidence in your relationships with women.

So, how do you adopt this positive, powerful position? It has to start from the very moment you first meet a woman. Every action and statement needs to position you as a person of value and power. You don't do this by being overpowering – you do it by being confident and consistent. Above all, don't be afraid of losing sex. More men cower from the position of power out of fear of losing physical closeness. Believe me, when you're in control, you'll have all the physical closeness you desire.

You can be sure that you are getting the test by answering the following questions:

- Does this seem like normal behavior? – No? You're getting the test.
- Does this seem like normal behavior for this woman? – No? You're absolutely getting the test.
- Do you feel defensive and/or confused by this reaction? – Yes? Unless you're very insecure, you're being tested.
- Does this seem to make sense in context of the situation? – No? Test city, baby!

Remember, you're going to have to anticipate the test to be in the best position to handle it. Don't assume that she'd never test *you* – after all, she's so sweet! This attitude will lead you right into test hell. You *will* be tested – no doubt about it.

OK, You're Getting The Test – What Do You Do?

How do you handle the test? In the same way you've already established your initial posture – firmly, directly and without hesitation. You will probably have to practice this, as it will not be the natural thing to do. You will not want to react by getting angry or by being confused. This is vital – you must not do either of these!

Now, it's time to get in touch with your "inner asshole." Don't worry about her reaction – it isn't important. She is testing *you*, not the other way around. Thus:

- Don't be afraid of losing her. First, you won't. Second, if you do, she wasn't worth it – believe me.
- Let her know that *you* know you're being tested. This helps prevent it in the future. She won't pull it again if she thinks she can't get away with it cleanly.
- Make an immediate assessment of the situation – what's the likely effect of failing this test? Will you be humiliated or embarrassed? Will you lose control of the situation? Are you going to have to "clean up" after her?
- Determine what is the most powerful position that you can take at that minute. What attitude will give you the most control and the most power?
- Take it! Don't be afraid to lose anything. React with calm confidence. Don't just fly off the handle. The more calculated your response, the better.
- Put the reaction back in *her* lap. Make her next action the determining one – make her have to move to succeed or fail.
- Decide with absolute resolve that you will walk if you don't get what *you* want.

It may also be helpful to find someone that you admire to act as a role model. When you're in a test situation, just think to yourself, "How would (your role model) handle this?" If you can't seem to find someone that you know personally, think of someone like John Wayne, or Michael Jordan, or someone else that you admire. Try to picture them in the same situation. How would they react?

Examples of Tests, and How To Handle Them

Here are some examples of some tests you may have to take.

You're out (or in) with your friends and she shows up unexpectedly.
Here, she is trying to make you look bad in front of your friends, showing that she has control over you – not them. You must not let this happen! Obviously, though

they may not say it, your friends will not be happy about it – would you? This is their time with you, and they deserve it. Further, they will begin to think that she *is* more important to you than they are. Remember, you may lose this girl someday, but your friends will always be there for you – if you treat them correctly.

Tell her, "You were not invited here and you know it." Her next reaction will be to get your friends to "vote" on her staying. This is a safe bet on her part, because first, your friends won't know if you really want the girl to stay, and second, they won't want to appear rude to your new squeeze. Thus, they'll always agree to her staying. Stop her (and them), and say, "No, I don't put my friends in the middle and neither will you. We'll have our time together later and as always, it will be special." Be adamant about it and send her away. Both she and your friends will find new respect for you.

The last step she may take is to be indignant about not being allowed to stay. Frankly, this will only happen about one time in five. But, if it does happen tell her, "My friends have the right to my time, just like you do. When it's your turn, I will pay attention only to you. When it's theirs, I will pay attention only to them." This is the end of discussion. Don't agree to continue it any further.

You two are in a public situation and she wants or does something inappropriate.

For example, you're at dinner with your boss, and she wants to kiss, she throws a tantrum, or she gets drunk at your friend or family's party. Any of these situations call for you to put her in her place. Excuse yourself and take her into a private area. Tell her absolutely that you will not tolerate this kind of behavior and if it happens again you'll put her in a cab and send her home.

Her next reaction is to get mad – don't be alarmed; this is part of the test. Go to the nearest telephone, or (even better), the hostess or manager of the restaurant and order a cab. Next, take her hand and go back to your boss, family member, friend, or whomever. Apologize for your date, as she'll be leaving now. You can explain the details to them later.

You must not get angry here; that is what she is looking for. You must remain calm and in control. Take her outside and wait for the cab to arrive. Now, this is very important – no matter what she says, no matter how she reacts, you must not give in. If she wants to walk home, let her. On the other hand, if she apologizes, or promises to behave, you will still send her home. Tell her, "I'm sorry, this situation is already handled. Once you've corrected this problem, I'll give you one more chance – but *not* before!"

She'll probably have enough time while waiting for the cab to try to convince you that she was only feeling left out, or that you've ignored her and that's why she misbehaved, or something similar. Here, she is trying to make you responsible for her actions. Don't let her do this! Continue to explain that the minute she tried to pull that behavior, she lost the right to feel slighted, rejected, or anything else. She is not the only one that was affected. You have the right to look good in the eyes of your friends, your boss, etc. Further, if she has an issue with you, it is only between you and her, and you'll be happy to discuss it later – in private.

You must not give in here. If you do, you will have lost, and she'll try to test you again sometime later. Once she realizes that you're not going to give in, she will probably even try to set the date of this next discussion!

She goes through your personal things

You didn't give her a key to your place, did you? What were you thinking? This is an invitation for her to dig up dirt on you. Unfortunately, it's really not her fault – she can't help this. Women are pre-programmed to be jealous and untrusting. The best way to handle this is to prevent it up front. Don't leave "incriminating" evidence lying around. Further, don't give her access to your place when you're not around.

Assuming that the damage is already done, she's going to find something and get angry with you for it. She'll find some other woman's love letters, panties or cologne, your porno collection, whatever. Her goal here is to put you on the defensive – stammering like an idiot – and force you to commit to something, like exclusivity to her.

The first step is to realize that you have an absolute right to privacy. She may not go through your things without your permission. As well, you may not go through her things either, since she has the same rights. The key here is to not become defensive. Remember that, no matter what she found, regardless of how incriminating it is, she did not have the right to look through your personal property. Focus on this. Say, "I'm sorry you feel the way you do, but that is totally null and void because *you* couldn't control yourself. You absolutely *do not* have the right to go through any of my stuff – now or ever. You have no idea what (the thing she found) means or doesn't mean." By the way, this may seem like a perfect time to get your key back; however, she probably has already made a copy of it, so you're going to need to change your locks. Please, please, don't assume that the key she gives you back is the only one – it isn't.

She wants to leave her personal things around your place

I call this "marking her territory." She wants to make your place look like there is another woman hanging around to tell any possible competitor that you're already taken. This may or may not meet with your goals, but in either case, it should be avoided. How you handle this one is crucial.

When you tell her "no," she's going to assume that you have other women coming over, and that is why she can't leave her things there. While this may be true, it doesn't give her the right to mark your personal space. This doesn't mean that she shouldn't have a drawer or two for her things. This way, when she spends the night, she has clothes readily available. She will also want to leave some of her toiletries. If you decide to allow this, request that she keep them in a particular drawer – not out on the counter. Frankly, after it's been there a few weeks you're going to forget about it – it's going to seem like a natural part of the room. Then, when Ms. Stripper comes over, she'll see these things and begin asking questions.

What she'll ask for is to reorganize your place (especially the bedroom and bathroom) with her things. There is no good reason (for you) to leave these out in the open. Thus, by giving her the drawer or two, you've effectively defeated this. If necessary, you can emphasize this by adding that, "Your things don't match my decor."

Once you've established that she cannot leave things out in the open at your home, she is going to try the next step – she will try to add a "woman's touch" to your place by "helping" you to redecorate. Unless you're an interior decorator or have a friend that is, you should consider letting her help you do this. Most women have a pretty good eye when it comes to these things. And, it will give you additional points with the next woman you bring over. Before you commit to letting her do this however, take a look at her place. If it is well decorated, go for it. If it is a mess, politely beg out of her help.

You're going to need a plan of action here. Decide just how feminine you're willing to go with this redecoration. Remember, the more feminine, the more it will look like another woman lives there. She'll tell you, "I want to put up new curtains here, a throw-rug over there, and repaint this room." Unless you have a real fondness for them, I suggest that you stop at fuzzy things in the bathroom or doilies on the coffee table. As well, stick with bolder, more masculine colors. Pastels are a dead giveaway, especially if they don't particularly match the other rooms.

She wants to know where "your relationship is going"
This often happens when you've set up a nice date, may have invested some money and she is trying to get you to prove that she is more important to you than your time and money. Simply tell her, "Dear, we're going into the theatre right now and this discussion isn't appropriate. You're very important to me, but this will have to wait until later when we can give it the proper attention." Next, tell her, "What if we go out for coffee right after the play and we'll discuss it then." You can give her any timeframe that you want – later that night, tomorrow, next week, whatever. The time isn't important, only that you commit to something. Don't wait for an answer. Just assume that she'll agree.

What she is really hoping is that your lack of preparation will cause you to commit to something beyond what you are willing to. The obvious answer here is to be prepared. Much easier said than done! Two people often view their relationship moving along at different speeds. She may be ready to commit to a monogamous relationship, and you may have just met a porn star!

This is one of the reasons that you want to schedule the time to discuss this. She wants you off guard, and off balance. You want to have thought out your response in advance. Don't agree to discuss something and then put it out of your mind until you do. You need to be prepared to field her questions, and respond with thoughtful answers. You can be vague here if it fits your needs. But, don't just react when she pulls this on you. You're going to wind up in trouble.

She leaves something out at her place for you to find

One device that women readily use is jealousy. They will try to make you jealous to pressure you into committing beyond your current willingness to do so. The best way to defuse this is to attack it head-on. Pick up the love note or photo set and read it, look over it. Then comment, "This is a lovely letter, I know exactly how he feels," or "You look so beautiful when you're in love." If you are the jealous type, you're best off just ignoring these things. Recognize that they are there and appreciate why – to get you to react.

If you find something really inciting like a pair of men's underwear, you can hardly avoid mentioning it, but try to defuse it rather than getting angry. Remember, she wants you off balance. That way, you can only react to something that she has already planned out. Say, "Uh-oh, it looks like your father left his underwear here!" You may find out that this really *is* her father's underwear – she was doing his laundry. On the other hand, if she tells you they belong to her "friend," you might say something like, "Oh, that's too bad – this place is only big enough for one pair of 'friend's' underwear," eluding to the fact that she is going to have to "clean up" her other relationships before she can have you. Then, drop it entirely – let her mull it over for a while. You may also want to make yourself unavailable for a while. If she thinks she has competition for your attention, she's going to have to work harder and drop the games altogether. In a case like this, there is no good reason to make it easy for her!

You are going to win here because: 1) she must want you or she wouldn't have done this, and 2) you've put it back in her lap. Now, she has to deal with the situation – and you've given her the tools to do this. If not today, very soon, she will say something like, "I've got room at my place for new underwear now," indicating that she is ready for your relationship to progress to the next point.

She "forgets" your date

Women don't "forget" dates (provided that you were clear on when and where the date was to be). There are two scenarios to consider; the first is when you meet her at her place, and the second is when she's supposed to meet you somewhere. Let's examine them separately.

You show up at her house, and she looks confused and isn't ready, but you're sure you've set the date for that time and place. Say to her, "You're not ready?" To which, she'll respond with something like, "Oh, I'm sorry, I didn't know that we had a date tonight!" or "I thought we were supposed to meet at 9:00, not 8:00!" You really have two choices here: either leave in a huff, or walk right in, sit down and tell her you'll wait, but to hurry up.

I recommend the second choice. You might even ask her, "Do you need some help selecting an outfit?" She probably won't, as she is going to act put out. Don't let her theatrics bother you. Act just as if she were on time and go out to have fun – regardless of her attitude. If she tries to give you a hard time, just ignore it and have fun with everyone else you meet. Talk to the waitress, the valet, and the couple at the table next to you. Eventually, she'll give in and start having fun too.

If you had dinner reservations, and you're afraid you're going to be late, you might say to her, "We have dinner reservations. Can you be ready in 10 minutes, or do you want to cook?" This is a very powerful position to take and doesn't give her much of a choice. She will probably take longer than 10 minutes to get ready as she is going to try to regain control. Thus, while she is dressing, quietly call the restaurant and reschedule the reservations for one-half to one hour later. She will respect you for not letting her get away with it.

In the second scenario, she is supposed to meet you at your place, or somewhere else, but doesn't show up, claiming that she "forgot." This is by far the worse of the two situations. You have a right to have your time respected (remember how busy you are). If she can't see this, I suggest that you dump this woman – don't call her back, let her call you. If you're absolutely sure that her transgression is legitimate (unlikely!), then let *her* make it up to *you*. Here's how: when she calls, tell her with some indignity, "I have very little time to waste and don't appreciate you forgetting our date. How are you going to make it up to me?" Then, be absolutely quiet. Do not say another word. The first one to speak loses.

She will now have to come up with something to make up for her mistake. This not only causes her to admit it, but also firmly anchors in her mind that you're not going to be treated this way. She will never forget again! She will next come up with another date – something like, "Well, let's go out next Wednesday?" or "Why don't I cook for you on Saturday?" Then, *hold her to it!* Remember, she is asking you out now, so say, "Where are you going to take me?" And, let her pay the check! If she invites you for dinner, say, "Okay, what time do you want me there?"

She doesn't call to cancel a date
This is a similar situation to the one above. Here, you show up and for some reason, she didn't bother to let you know that she is sick, or had an aunt die unexpectedly, or was called into work. You have to make it absolutely clear that you will not accept this type of behavior. Your time is extremely valuable and limited, and she doesn't have the right to waste it.

Obviously, be sensitive and concerned for her problem, but be adamant. If she wants to see you again, you'll allow her to call *you* and set the next date. After all, you've already done the work here once and she took advantage of *you*. Women hate this because they aren't very good at setting dates. Consider also, that because of this, she may never call you! In this case, it's no loss on your part. If she does call you, you can bet she'll never forget to call you again!

She flirts with other men when on a date with you
This is very insidious. Most men just blow it off, thinking, "Oh, she's just outgoing." Don't you believe it! When she is with you, you deserve 100% of her attention. Likewise, she deserves 100% of your attention too – don't flirt with other women while you're with her either.

Let's look at this more closely. How do you know when this happens? Sometimes it is blatant, sometimes more subdued. For example, if she turns her back to you at a bar and spends more than just a few sentences talking with another man without including you in the conversation, you're being ignored. If she goes off dancing with other men and leaves you by yourself, you're being ignored. If she sees a friend of hers (male or female) and runs off to the table to talk and spends more than a moment or two, especially without introducing you, you're being ignored.

By the way, for this reason, never agree to take her to her favorite hangout – at least for the first four or five dates! She probably has been there many times before with her friends and knows both the employees and the regulars. She may go off flirting with all the people she knows, leaving you at the table looking stupid. Also, if you take her dancing, don't go off and dance with anyone else, even if she doesn't want to dance. This is rude and tells her that you're not really interested in her – whether you are or not. Wait until you're with your buddies and come back later if this is a prime "Betty" hangout.

So, how do you handle this situation? As with the other examples, specifically, directly and to the point. Say to her, "When you're with me, you're on *my* time. If that isn't good enough for you, then you'd better make sure that there's somebody else here who'll take you home, because I'm outta here!" If you want to add strong emphasis to this, lean over to the guy that she was talking with (make sure that she can hear you!), and say, "Do you want to take her home?" Then, without waiting for a response from either of them, get up and walk out. She'll be running after you like a lost puppy.

She'll react in one of two ways; either with anger, "I was only *talking* to him!" or apologetically, "Oh, I'm sorry – I didn't mean to hurt your feelings." In either case tell her, "I'm here with you because I want to be here with you. You may treat other men that way, but I expect the same courtesy and respect I give you – period." Next, wait for a sincere apology from her.

She unexpectedly includes others in your time together (like kids or friends)
You've just set up a date to do something and when you arrive she answers the door with, "Look who just got into town – my friend from Washington; she can come along with us, right?" Depending on what you had planned, maybe she can or maybe she can't join the two of you. Remember, her friend didn't just show up, she had to know that this friend was coming to town. So you've got to handle this like the affront that it is.

For example, if you have expensive tickets to a show or you're planning to make your move under this woman's skirt, you probably don't want her friend around. In this case, say to her, "You know, I've planned an evening for us to be together – just the two of us. I expect to be consulted *before* the plans change. You'll either have to find a way to entertain your friend while we go out, or I'll go without you." Then, stick to it.

If the situation isn't as clear-cut as the above examples, you'll have to determine what you want to do. For example, if you and she were just going shopping together, or were going to a party, you can invite the extra person along, if you feel it is appropriate.

In all of these scenarios, you'll notice that the key is to control your anger. Her goal is to make you angry or jealous. You must learn to control this and react in a calm, cool and thoughtful way. Do this, and you'll beat the test every time.

General Guidelines on Test-Passing

Men, you can't avoid the test. It is going to come whether you like it or not. Your only defense is a good offense. Get in touch with this fact right now. You're going to have to learn to pass the test to be successful with women in the long run.

However, you can ensure that the test you get will be: 1) easier for you to pass; and 2) the last test you will need to pass. Here's how you do this:

- Be calm – don't just react! This is exactly what she is expecting from you.
- Think through the situation clearly (and quickly!). Determine the most powerful position you can take at that exact moment.
- Put the onus on her to correct the problem – don't try to be the problem solver. She is trying to get you to jump through some hoop. Don't do it!
- Remember that you are due proper respect and courtesy. Most of all tests revolve around you losing one or both of these.
- Resolve absolutely that you will not accept mistreatment in any form.
- Absolutely avoid violence of any type – mental, verbal, or physical.

What if You Fail The Test?

Why did you fail? Go back and reread this chapter. If you're coming to this section after you've been tested, there may be something you can do to resurrect the situation. First, make sure that you have a good grasp of the previous information on handling tests. Second, recognize that trying to re-handle the test after it's been given is not very effective. Third, you'll probably get another test anyway (provided that she didn't dump you out of lack of respect for you!).

Thus, to try to correct a failed test, you can do the following:

Evaluate what she really wanted you to do to pass the test.
For example, did she want you to stand up to her? Did she want you to take control? Did she want something that you didn't provide?

Make sure that you're in a position of power before proceeding.
Don't try to bring the issue back up just after sex, or when she is angry with you. You'll just appear scared that you're going to lose her or that you're insincere and trying to appease her anger. Wait until things are settled down and you're with her in a quiet, comfortable and private setting.

Re-address the situation with her, and apologize for not handling it properly.
What? Apologize? Yes – tell her, "Honey, I've been thinking about that situation that happened yesterday over dinner. You know, I didn't think about what exactly was going on and reacted poorly. In looking back at the situation, I see now that you didn't really want me to (fill in the blank), you were really testing me to see how I would react!"

Now, she isn't going to admit to this. Thus, just keep saying with confidence, "No, it's okay – I understand."

Tell her that next time, you'll handle it differently.

Explain that you expect certain things from her such as respect and courtesy, and that these were not given, but that you understand what she really wanted from you.

Wait for the next test and be ready!

Unfortunately, this is not the best situation you could have. It is far better to handle the test when it occurs rather than having to regroup after a failure. Bringing this back up will let her know that you are aware of what she was doing and may prevent it in the future. But, please don't rely on this, as it is as unlikely as your brother just "forgetting" about that loan he gave you. You'd better be ready for your next test – and pass it!

The Rules

Whether you like it or not, you've been lied to. You don't have to take my word for it. Just look around you. If you watch television, you'll find that men are portrayed as bumblers, fools, abusers, adulterers, homosexuals, and rapists. If you read magazines, you'll find that advertising geared toward men demeans and insults us. Have you looked at a billboard lately? Heard a radio program recently? Listened in on a conversation between two or more women? Seen a "chick flick" within the past 10 years?

Men are being told that we are the cause of the world's problems. We are the reason why so many women are unhappy. It's because of us that we lost the Mars Polar Lander. Whatever. It's time to open our male eyes and see just what is going on around us. Go rent "My Best Friend's Wedding" or "Mrs. Doubtfire" and see how male roles are being portrayed.

These are the kinds of rules you live with. They are designed to place you in a reduced status – to give you a handicap. Popular opinion states that men have enjoyed the majority of benefit in our society and therefore must be burdened to balance the scales. Obviously, in different arenas, others are faced with their own rules too: women, majorities, minorities, soccer teams, etc., all have their own rules. I find the rules for men very menacing however because they are seen as "cute," "charming," and something we are supposed to fight through.

Let me state clearly right now, I am absolutely against any form of violence between men and women that is non-consensual. Whatever you do in your bedroom is none of my business as long as it is consensual. However, men are not abusers or batterers by nature. I had the following conversation with an ex-girlfriend about a year ago that, believe it or not, actually counsels people in relationships:

Her: I live in constant fear of being abused.
Me: Why do you feel that way? I have never hit you or even raised my hand in anger to you even once in our relationship, have I? (Note: we'd been together for about two years by that time).
Her: No, *you* never have, but you know that most men are abusive.
Me: Huh? Most men are abusive? Where did you get that?
Her: It's a fact!
Me: You are saying that more than 50% of men abuse women.
Her: Yes, that's what I'm saying.
Me: Have you been abused by half of the men you've dated?
Her: Well no, but most women have.
Me: How do you know that? Where did you get that statistic?
Her: It's a well-known fact – everybody knows it.

Obviously, this conversation continued on long into the night. I bring it up here because this is one attitude that you as a man face every day. Both popular culture and popular media consistently make you out to be the bad guy. But it doesn't stop there. Every time you begin a relationship with a woman, you are being eyed as a potential devil or potential savior. "Will he cheat on me?" "Will he abuse me or my kids?" "Will he steal from me?" Or, "Will he help me out of the financial hole I'm in?" "Will he send my kids to college?" "Will he buy me a nice house, or some nice jewelry?" "Will he take me to Europe?"

Further, a very large number of women live their lives right into the ground in the hopes that the "Knight in Shining Armor" will come along and make everything better – pay the bills, handle the ex-husband, put the kids through college, etc. You, my friend, are the target of all this, and you'd better know it up front. Because of this, you need to protect yourself. You need to have a clear understanding of what is involved in your relationships with women. That is the purpose of this chapter.

Now, let's explore other rules that you and I have to live with (or at least, had better know).

Rule #1 – Women control the sex.

This is a critically important rule to understand. Women control the sex, and therefore they also control the speed of the relationship. You do not. They also believe that, because they control the sex, and you want the sex, that they control **you**. The fact is, in too many relationships, whether starting off or long-term, they're right.

Rule #2 – A women sizes you up within a few minutes and knows if she will sleep with you or not.

Sad, but true. You're ready to sleep with any woman that fits a broad profile of attractiveness for you. She is going to be much more discriminating and careful. Further, she won't tell you this up front.

Rule #3 – Regardless of her intentions, she'll let you spend your money, time, and attention on her.

How many times have you met a woman in a social setting like a bar, gotten to know her a little, maybe even bought her a few drinks, only to have her say, "well, I've got to go now," and she turns and walks out without even giving you her phone number? Or, worse yet, you actually take a woman out on a few dates (usually at $100 or more each), and never sleep with her? Frankly, it is usually much less expensive and more expedient to hire a prostitute.

Women know that you are pre-inclined to do these things in an attempt to impress them. This *doesn't* impress them, by the way. Further, there is little if any stigma in a woman accepting such gratuities. On the other hand, if you, as a man do this, you are looked down on as having "used" the woman! Don't be a jerk! Stop spending that money that you work so hard for. You don't need to spend much (if anything) to get what you want. We'll discuss how to do this later, but for right now – **just stop!**

Rule #4 – There are many generally accepted double standards that you live with.

For example, when a man hits a woman it is an abomination. If a woman hits a man, it is acceptable! (We'll deal with this particular scenario later, but I want to state clearly here, that I don't think that anyone should hit anyone else for any reason). I've seen some pretty severe damage done to men after being hit by women with big rings on their hands or having something large thrown at them. Criminal behavior? You bet! But, after one of my friends was hit in the face with a fork by his (ex) girlfriend, the doctor actually said, "See – you really shouldn't piss them off!" What would he have said if it were the girlfriend that had been injured?

Rule #5 – Men are *not* monogamous.

Popular culture would have you believe that you meet the woman of your dreams (by some sheer stroke of luck), you fall madly in love and get married, happily for the rest of your life. Maybe your parents or grandparents did this. Then again, maybe not. Make no mistake about it; you're living in a different world than your parents or grandparents.

The fact is you're probably going to run into *many* women of your dreams. Today, most of the U.S. population live in large metropolitan cities, and thus, have access to a much larger body of dateable women than the smaller agricultural communities around at the turn of the 20th century and before. But really, what difference does this make? Let's examine the facts.

Although men are not monogamous, they can *choose* to be. I have made this statement to many people over the past few years and seem to get the same types of reactions from both men and women. Popular thinking says that men and women *should* be monogamous. They state that this is best for so many reasons – the family, the church, the country – but they never really consider the facts.

Women often complain about their man's eye getting caught by every pretty skirt that walks by. "Are you even listening to me?" they ask with contempt. As men, we understand that we look at women – even lust for women – regularly. However, we usually decide to stick with one for many reasons.

This "searching" behavior is present in every man that has reached puberty. We get pleasure from looking at women. Women also like to look at men (and usually other women as well – explaining the predominance of sexually oriented advertisements of females in women's magazines). However, they don't "size up" a man as potential mates in the same way men do. They are usually more concerned with the condition of the present relationship than considering the next one.

Everybody wants to believe that humans have evolved beyond their early instincts and in some ways we have. We carry this desire to believe further than is factual, however. The fact is, in humans and animals, males are best off siring young with many females in order to assure that some will survive and carry on their genes. Females on the other hand attempt to form longer-term relationships with the fathers of their children in order to increase the chance for survival of the entire family. Further, by concentrating only on the few children they have, they can help to ensure their survival.

Our early ancestors promoted this model as the only way they could assure that their kind continued to exist. The females would bear and raise the young while the male would hunt for food. The females often supplemented this limited food supply as well by gathering what they could, but the ultimate responsibility fell on the males. Some feel that women's "gatherer" instincts help to explain their almost unanimous love of shopping – it seems to satisfy something very primitive inside them.

Rule #6 – Women *want to be* monogamous.

For many of the reasons stated previously, women are, or want to be monogamous. Women's magazines promote this very heavily. In fact, most women define their success or failure by their relationships with men – a good relationship equates to success, a bad relationship to failure.

Women also have other reasons for wanting to be monogamous. First, by staying with one man, they get to reap the benefits of that man's success. Like their children, by concentrating their efforts on their partner, they can help to induce his success ("behind every successful man…") and, of course, benefit through his doing well. Second, in many cultures, and up to about 20 years ago in this country, cheating by women carried a very heavy stigma. It is actually against the law in many cultures for women to stray – and can carry a death penalty! This stigma continues in some ways today. It is looked at in women as an inability to maintain a relationship – very bad to womankind.

Rule #7 – Women spend their entire lives learning the art of the relationship and are therefore better at it than you are.

I have asked a number of men and women a simple question – "Did your [parent of the same sex] ever give you any relationship advice?" Of the 49 men I've asked this question, 100% of them said, "No." Of the 56 women I've asked, all but one said, "Yes." Now, 105 is not a representative figure of the overall population, but this vast difference between the sexes does raise some important questions. Why does it seem that all of the men of whom I asked this question are not getting the benefit of their father's relationship experience? Further, why are most of the women getting their mother's?

Of course, this isn't the only evidence I'm using to set this rule. If you look at any publication, television program, movie or talk show aimed at women, you will see that they concentrate mostly on relationship information. They spend hours dissecting and exploring every possible aspect of women's relationships – with their men, their mothers, their fathers, their bosses, their employees, their doctors, etc. For men, this is difficult – even painful – to watch. We find it tedious and boring.

We are often confused by women's responses to things that seem very straightforward to us. Sometimes they are amazed at us for not having better ways to deal with our relationship problems. They often feel that we have far more limited relationship skills (we usually do!). They also sometimes believe that because of this, we are simpler than they are. Nothing could be farther from the truth! We are by nature, highly complex and evolved. We had to be intuitive communicators to survive. Our male ancestors used very subtle facial and auditory cues to communicate aspects of a hunt, for example. Further, our methods of dealing with relationships are more ingrained and tend to reflect our approach to the rest of our world.

When you deal with women, you'll have to make a choice. Do you want to deal with them on their ground (unwise), or yours (very wise)? Women usually react emotionally to situations. We men on the other hand, consider most situations in a logical, results-oriented way. Your women will want to dissect all of the emotions of the issue while you will want to consider the facts only and move on to the solution.

However, be aware that in order to be successful you must understand how women view and deal with relationships. It really isn't as hard as it first seems. They have specific patterns that you can learn to recognize easily. Then, you can create an approach for each of these patterns.

Rule #8 - Western marriage and Valentine's Day are for women – not men.

Doubt this rule? Look at the difference in the price of the wedding gown compared to the tux rental or purchase. Look at all the traditions – they are aimed at the women. Look at the entire wedding process – there are magazines for brides, there are entire books about the wedding process, there are talk shows about the wedding, all geared toward women. Little girls begin planning their weddings very early. They dream of huge, white weddings where all eyes are on the bride. What will the bridesmaids wear? What music will they play? Who will be invited? What kind of flowers?

On the other hand men are almost superfluous to the process. We show up dressed in our tux and recite a few lines, pose for pictures and make nice for the family. Except for the bachelor party, which is male-focused, the rest of the wedding process is exclusively for our women. In fact, most aspects of the marriage are women-focused. Think about the marriages you know.

Valentine's Day is another women-oriented experience. It is quickly becoming a yearly attempt for men to find the "perfect" gift. Not only are men less interested in the day, they are also expected to excel in the expression of the meaning of the day – the love of their women. Let the day go by without finding that perfect gift for your gal and watch the excitement! You'll have an entire year's worth of material to savor.

Rule #9 – Every aspect of our society is directed toward supporting women in their relationships against men.

Our society has evolved under the belief that women are weaker and less capable than men and therefore, we owe them special consideration. Everything from popular culture to our divorce courts direct their focus to women's needs over men's. Here are just a few examples:

- Men have little or no say in a woman's right to choose to give birth.
- In some states, even if someone other than the husband fathers a child, the husband becomes financially responsible for the child.
- Many women (and men!) feel that it is okay to accept financial support, gifts, money, and so on, from men, stating, "After all – they are getting *me*!"
- Women almost always automatically receive alimony in divorce situations (referred to by a local radio personality as "vaginamony").
- In the vast majority of cases, women get primary custody of children in divorces.
- In almost every case, when a woman claims any form of battery (whether actual battery has occurred or not), the man is instantly suspect.

This list goes on and on. It illustrates my point – until society becomes more equitable in its thinking, you have to deal with the unfair status in which you live.

Rule #10 – Your looks don't really matter.

No doubt you've seen some gorgeous women hanging on the arm of an ugly, obese, or aged man. In fact, this is so common that it really isn't a stretch to say that you probably know people like this. How can this be? Don't attractive women want to be with attractive guys? Of course they do. But, this often isn't the most important issue for them.

I've heard this from many beautiful women. They say that they have trouble getting dates. What, you say? How could a beauty have trouble finding dates? Most men are afraid to approach these women. Somehow they seem out of range.

A number of years ago, I was sitting in an out-of-town club with a few of my male friends. We were all eyeing the local talent when in walked a women so beautiful, she could make a Bishop kick in a stained glass window. All of my friends' jaws dropped to the floor (as did mine!). Two other girls of lesser, but still respectable looks accompanied her and they sat at a table across the room.

As my friends and I talked and danced with other women at the bar, these girls ordered drinks and sat conversing with each other. One of my friends (a male model) kept saying that he'd love to meet "Ms. Beauty," but wasn't going to ask her. I couldn't believe it, and asked him why. He responded, "She's really hot – she probably has a boyfriend." I asked him if he was sure of his decision, and he said yes. So I got up and walked over to their table, apologized for interrupting them and ask Ms. Beauty to dance. She looked surprised as she accepted the invitation.

We danced for a while and we then returned to my table to meet my friends. Soon, her other friends were invited to join us and we all drank and danced. Ms. Beauty and I finally left, had dinner and went back to my hotel room for the evening.

Remember, you don't have the right to make decisions for your prospective woman. Let her make her own; you just have to make the first move.

Rule #11 – You have to become marketable.

Who would want to try to sell something nobody wanted to buy? That would be stupid. Thus, you're going to have to make yourself market-ready. This really isn't as difficult as it first sounds. You will explore this rule in much greater detail later in this book, but for now, just keep in mind that you're going to have to be someone that your prospective woman wants to be with. However, consider Rule #10 – you don't have to be Leonardo DiCaprio, just presentable.

Rule #12 – If you haven't slept with a women after four or five dates, you're probably not going to – ever!

Actually, I believe in the "three-date" rule – if you haven't slept with her after three legitimate dates, forget it. I mentioned back in Rule #1 that women control the sex – not you. As in Rule #2, a women knows almost immediately if she *is* going to sleep with you or not. Further, as per Rule #3, she won't hesitate to let you lavish her with money, gifts, your time, dinners, and attention, even if she doesn't plan to sleep with you.

Do you really think that the woman you're with that won't bang you doesn't know your real intention? Don't be a jerk. Of course she does. Drop her *right now* and go find a woman that respects you and understands that both you *and* she have goals. Then, don't spend a fortune trying to get into her pants either!

Rule #13 – The women you're attracted to speak a different language.

This rule is so important it probably should have gone first. You are going to have to learn to speak the language of the woman you want. Fortunately, it's a lot like English. Unfortunately, it's a lot different from the English *you* speak right now. Further, you're going to have to teach your woman to speak *your* language as well. They aren't likely to know it right off the bat.

Why do women and men speak different languages? The easiest answer is that they are coming from different motivations. What women want from their experience with men is somewhat different from what men want. Thus, they express themselves in ways that meet those needs. Keep in mind that there are women that want a lot of what you want. However, in the context of relationships, these women will tend to make a better friend for you than a lover. We will see how this is so in the chapter on communications.

Rule #14 – You can't convince anyone to do anything.

This is an important rule. If you are reading this book to try to learn how to convince that blonde in accounting to go out with you, you're probably reading the wrong book. If instead, you want to make yourself more interesting in her eyes, you're on the right track. It's far better (and easier) to get her to chase you than to try convincing her that she should be with you. We'll see how a little later.

Rule #15 – You need to decide specifically what you want.

If you're happy taking whatever comes along, then this book isn't for you. If you don't plan your life, it is going to be open to the whim of everyone else that you meet. Their planning will become yours. I really like the old saying, "If you don't stand for something you'll fall for anything." People spend vast amounts of time listening to and simply adopting the opinions of others. Think not? What do churches promote? They advocate a single doctrine that each follower is expected to accept and embody. How many of those followers then sit down to consider exactly what their church promotes and how it fits in their own belief structure? It seems to me a better choice would be to decide *first* what you believe and then find a church that promotes that belief.

This is only one example of many available. The point here is that; if you want to be truly successful in all areas of your life, make decisions about it for yourself! Don't simply take what others give you, (including what's in this book), and adopt it because it sounds good. Be a student, not a follower! Use the information so readily available to you to craft your belief system. Then, make clear and specific decisions about your life. Finally, put those decisions into action.

Rule #16 – You'll have to go through a number of women (possibly a large number) to find what you want.

You must accept the fact that, to find what you're looking for, you'll need access to a lot of women. Further, you're going to have to date a large number of them to be sure you've found what you want! If you don't do this, you'll have to settle with whoever just happens along – if anyone.

I'm not stating that you'll have to develop relationships with many women. In fact, I recommend that you become this involved with very few. There is nothing wrong with being discriminating; after all, the women you are after are doing this. In a later section we'll look at how to determine which women fit your goals, and which ones to avoid.

Fortunately, you have a real advantage here. First, more than half of the population is female. Second, they are all around you. Third, once you've established your goals and created your plan, they are going to find *you*, (with your help, of course!)

Rule #17 – You'll have to learn how to make love to a woman.

Every man I've talked to says that he *knows* how to make love to a woman. Most women I talk to tell me that their men really *don't* know how to make love to them. Who is right? In this case, I tend to take the side of the women. When you consider the amount of material available to men on what women want, it is absurd that so many men *think* they know what women want and so few really seem to.

There's something about this that has always bothered me. If these women are dissatisfied with their lover, why don't they help them? Women tend to think that we men should just know intuitively what they want. Most of the time, we assume that they want just what we want – to our own peril! The fact is, most women won't tell you what they want, let alone offer any instruction.

Decide right now that you're going to spend the rest of your life perfecting your techniques. Commit to it. There is little so rewarding as becoming an expert in satisfying your women. Further, if you too want to find the highest level of satisfaction possible for yourself (both in sex and your relationships with women), this is the key.

The first step to being the best lover you can be is to drop the attitude that you already know how to screw. Putting it in and getting off may be the goal, but there is so much more both before *and* after. Frankly, you may not want a repeat performance with the woman you just spent an evening with. Fine. But realize this – women talk. And, they talk about **you**. Depending on your available pool of women, you may one day or another run into someone that knows this woman. Why not come from a point of respect and anticipation from the new woman rather than suspicion or even contempt?

If, on the other hand you are looking to repeat the act one or more times, you'd better make it worthwhile for her. As I mentioned before, don't assume that you're channeling Casanova's sexual energy. Set out now to improve your skills. As you become a better lover, your lovers will get better too! (Yes, I promise!)

How do you go about becoming a better lover? Read, watch, ask, and most important – listen. Your present (or last) woman is a wealth of information. Your next woman will also help you, if you know how to ask. Men assume that sexual skill is inborn – that it comes from their genes. Sorry, it is a skill to develop, pure and simple. You should never be ashamed to ask specifically what a woman wants. Then, try it and have her help you become even better. Would it bother you if she asked what *you* wanted?

Communication Models

Psychologists use models to better understand human behavior. These models (of which there are many) help to predict what people may do or say, and what they mean when they communicate. Some models also help to answer the question, "Why did he/she do that?" An understanding of some of these models will help to improve your relationship skills. Below, we'll explore a few of the more popular and effective communication models. The better you become at understanding and using these models, the better you will be at selling yourself. Perhaps even more important, you'll become better at interpreting what a woman is really saying.

A few caveats are appropriate here before we discuss some of the communication models:

No one person is exactly like any of the models presented. We are all a blend of experiences, beliefs, morals and ethics, lessons, and emotions. It is for this reason that I present more than one model. Each gives a slightly different picture of a person, and by combining them together the picture becomes more accurate.

Models are organized into categories. Categories describe a foundational, working element of the model. People will fall into one or more categories in the model structures, and all models apply to all people. However, like the models themselves, very few people are 100% of any category of any model. Usually less than one percent of people will be exactly like the category presented. Instead, they will often be a mixed percentage of two or more categories, or will fall somewhere in between 0–100%. Each model represents a slightly different picture. Thus, you may find that one model fits well in certain circumstances, but won't apply in others.

You should understand each model fully before trying to apply it to your program. By not completely understanding how the communication model works, you will likely misuse it, and thus, your success will be reduced. Also, you will find that practice in applying a model will greatly help your understanding and use of it.

You will probably find that one of the models fits better with your experience. I encourage you to learn them all, but use the models that are most effective for you. Further, you will probably want to apply different models to different situations. However, one of the models will probably make the most sense. Become an expert in that model!

Finally, use yourself and your own experiences as a guide when considering the models.

The Male Versus Female Model

Face the facts – women communicate differently than men. This model deals with these communication differences. To be more specific, the differences in communication between men and women come from their motivations. Men tend to be motivated by the outcome (goal-oriented); women tend to be motivated by the content (emotion-oriented).

These differences usually don't pose significant problems in day-to-day communications. On the other hand, consider a fight. This is where tempers are flared, and people will revert to their most comfortable, fundamental communication styles. Men generally will want to review the issues of the problem and find a solution. Women want to spend their time exploring the details of the interaction. It is for this reason that men often feel that women don't listen to them ("We already *have* a solution – why do you want to go on and on?"), and women feel that men don't listen to them ("You're not *hearing* what I'm saying!"). In actuality, both men and women are really saying, "I'm not getting what I want from this conversation!"

Why aren't they getting what they want? Because the things they want aren't apparent to the other person. Each person wants their needs met, and they expect the other person to know what those needs are. Frankly, neither of them usually knows what the other wants.

When women ask for attention, they usually just want us to listen and be supportive. However, men are problem solvers. Thus, we react with an immediate answer to the issue. For example, she says, "I'm feeling like I don't contribute anything at work." He responds, "Why not find a why to save money on office supplies?" She gets angry; he gets confused. Wait, didn't she just tell me that she is having a problem at work? Yes, she did – technically. However, what she is asking for is your attention to her feelings. Right now, she isn't concerned about a solution – only a person to listen while she vents.

When men talk to their women, they are much more likely to deal with specifics. For example, we say, "Honey, I had the worst meeting with my boss today." She responds with, "Oh, poor baby, are you angry about it?" How infuriating! We are ready to detail our plan of attack of how we're going to deal with the situation and may even ask for her ideas. All she wants to do is hear how angry or hurt we are!

Sometimes, we men just need to get away from our women and be on our own, or with our buddies. It is usually right about this time when she says, "I want to talk." (I can feel the hair on the back of your neck standing up!) It seems that the more we pull away the more they chase us (important key here!). Women need to understand that we sometimes have to distance ourselves from our relationships.

This doesn't mean that we are breaking them off – just recharging ourselves. We need to understand that what is a natural part of our communication model, is seen by women as a threat to their relationships with us.

The Motivation Model

This model is based on a highly simplified "Myers-Briggs Personality Survey" model (originally proposed by Carl Jung [1875-1961]). It breaks personality types down into four categories (known as "modalities"):

- Director
- Socializer
- Intellectual
- Amiable

You can view the relationship of these modalities as follows:

	Facts Oriented	Relationship Oriented
Active Personality Types	Director	Socializer
Passive Personality Types	Intellectual	Amiable

As mentioned earlier, very few people fit entirely within any one category. Such a person would be at the outer corner of their respective type. As a person's type moves closer toward one edge or another, they begin to acquire more of the attributes of the type near that edge. For example, if a person is sitting in the middle of the director's box, they are 50% director, 25% socializer, and 25% intellectual; if they are in the center of the socializer's box, they are 50% socializer, 25% intellectual, and 25% amiable. If they are right at the intersection of the four types, they are 25% director, 25% socializer, 25% intellectual and 25% amiable.

Note that (as you will see in the other models), people move between the modalities, but only right-left or up-down – almost never diagonally. For example, in some situations a director is likely to be either social or intellectual (or both); an intellectual can be a director or an amiable, and so on. However, socials almost never become intellectuals, nor do amiables become directors. These types are usually in too great a conflict with the motivation of the person.

Let's look at how the types relate:

Active Versus Passive Types

This chart shows the extreme patterns of these types – that is, how they deal with their worlds when exclusively within that modality. Keep in mind that not every one will have every attribute, nor will anyone have them all the time:

	Active	Passive
Speed of Speech	Fast, animated	Slow, thoughtful
Social Focus	Outward	Inward
General Reactions	Reactionary	Purposeful
Personal Interaction with Others	High	Low
Acceptance of Others	High	Low
Understanding of Self	High	Low
Appearance	Clean, neat	Disheveled, unkempt

Facts Versus Relationship Types

This is fairly easy to understand – generally the facts-oriented person deals better with information and detail, while the relationship-oriented person deals better with people and their feelings toward them or their interpretation of how others feel about them. You can also think of this as a "focus." Relationship folks view their worlds by their relationship with others (external focus). Facts folks view their worlds by their person interpretation (internal focus).

Examining the Modalities

Now that you have an understanding of the motivating factors for each personality type, let's look at the specifics of each modality:

Director
This person is concerned with getting the job done. You might think of a director of a corporation as an example. They are highly goal/accomplishment-oriented. They are often not as interested in all the facts as they are in the accomplishments. They will take charge when needed, and are usually willing to work with others to get what they want.

Socializer
This person is concerned with the relationship between the parties. Often the "social butterfly," this person is the one who is introducing everyone at the party. They are generally well liked because they make you feel at ease.

Intellectual
This person is the one that wants information. Many of your college professors fall into this category. When they buy, they buy because it makes sense. Thus, they need a lot of information to make the right choice. However, don't think that they don't get excited. When the information is overwhelmingly positive toward a particular value, they jump.

Amiable
This person is the slow, methodical type. They ponder every word said, and watch to see what your reaction to them is. They are often willing to change their opinion if it doesn't suit you (especially if it isn't important), and want to "just get along."

The Neuro-Linguistic Programming Model

This model views people's communication in three modalities – visually, auditorally (hearing), and kinesthetically (touch, taste and smell). It also says that people have a prime modality – that is, one that they spend most of their time in, and a secondary modality – the one that they prefer to use when not using the prime. They can also use their tertiary modality, though not as often.

Thus, people move between the modalities. So, how do you know which modality someone is in at any particular moment? If you said "observation," you're absolutely right. By observing a person's actions and listening to their speech, you will determine where they are right at that moment. By watching and listening over a period of time, you will soon learn the primary and secondary modality. Why do you want to know what their modality is? Because you want to mirror it! (See the section ahead on "Applying the Model" for specifics.) You want your prospect to identify with you, connect and feel close to you.

The Visual Woman

This is the easiest woman to spot. She usually dresses very well, wears appropriate jewelry, and will even try to dress *you*! This is a compliment from the visual woman – she is molding the object of her affection to match her world. You will notice that her home is usually neat and well organized. Things match. Further, they will make sense together – just as you and she will – when you "look right."

The visual woman uses visual language; phrases such as, "I see what you mean" or "That looks good to me." Visual words are a dead giveaway, but don't rely on them alone. Another real language key is rapid speech. When a visual woman is speaking it is usually pretty fast.

You should also watch her eyes. Do they dart around the room? Does she seem to be "looking" for her thoughts? If you want to be absolutely sure she is visual (you *do* want to be sure, don't you?), ask her an open-ended question and note how she tries to answer. I like to ask, "What do you remember most about your childhood?" or "What do you remember about the house you grew up in?" If she is visual, she will try to "go there" by looking straight up or up and to the side. She is trying to "see" the thoughts of her childhood or visualize her house. Be careful not to ask her a question in your own modality. For example, you wouldn't want to ask her, "Do you remember seeing that movie _____ when you were a child?" (visual), "What was your favorite song when you were growing up?" (auditory), or "How did you feel about your family when you were young?" (kinesthetic).

The Auditory Woman

To the auditory woman, the world is full of sounds. You can't really use her dress or jewelry as a good indicator here as she may just be very good at selecting her clothes. Instead, you have to ask her questions and listen to the answers. If she regularly uses phrases like, "I hear you," "That rings a bell," or "Sounds like a plan," you are probably with an auditory woman.

Again, you can use the speed of her speech as a guide. It will be neither fast nor slow, but somewhere in between. She will definitely use "sound" words. Also, watch her eyes as you ask her the open-ended question. If they move straight across toward her ears, you've got an auditory woman.

For example, you ask her, "What do you remember most about your childhood?" to which she responds, "Well, we had this little church right down the road that would ring its bells every hour. When I heard those bells, I always knew I was home." Or, "My mom used to play her records hour after hour and we'd just sit and listen or dance sometimes."

The Kinesthetic Woman

The kinesthetic woman is feelings-based (I'm not referring to emotions – all women work in emotion). They use language like, "This doesn't feel right," "Something smells fishy about that," or "You've touched a part of me." When they respond to your open-ended questions, they often will look down at the table or their laps trying to search their souls for the answers. Also, they speak very slowly and deliberately. This last item is a dead giveaway.

Remember that with all of these modalities, women often move through more than one of them. They will often unconsciously adopt *your* modality (or the one you're presently in), trying to connect with you. Thus, a single clue will not be enough for you to determine a woman's prime modality. You need to get multiple clues. Give yourself some time, and practice. Use the techniques presented later under "Applying the Model" to gauge your success.

The Sexuality Model

This model comes from hypnotherapy. A number of years ago, practitioners of hypnosis began noticing that their subjects often used language consistent with the way they viewed the world deep down in their subconscious. Their language types also seemed to reflect their modes of dress, their style, the amount of jewelry they wore, and the way they carried themselves. This became known as "sexuality." Note that, while a woman's sexual personality is part of this model, it is only one aspect. As used here, it refers to everything done or expressed outwardly.

Further, by using the proper language, hypnotists could help induce desired actions more efficiently. This is known as "suggestibility." Do you need to hypnotize your woman to use this model? No, but if you'll use the information presented here, you'll find hypnosis-like attention from women in your communications.

This model uses the following scale:

Emotional:	100%	50%	0%
	----------------------------	----------------------------	
Physical:	0%	50%	100%

To use this scale, a person's sexuality is designated by a line placed at the appropriate point on the scale. Like the other modalities, very few people are 100% emotional or 100% physical. Most people are less than this. Here's how this scale works – if you're 25% emotional, you are 75% physical; if you're 52% emotional, you are 48% physical, and so on. The higher a person exists on either side of this scale, the more like the examples given below that person will be.

Now, what does it mean to be physically or emotionally sexual? It doesn't mean that emotionals cry a lot, or that physicals are going to jump you the first chance they get. In fact, physicals are more likely to express their emotions outwardly (e.g., through crying, laughing, touching) where emotionals will try to keep them hidden. This gets a little tricky, so stay with me here.

Emotional people tend to feel more at home with their emotions. Further, they use them to protect their physical bodies. Have you ever gone up to a woman to hug her and had her react in a way that makes you stop? You probably tried to hug an emotional-sexual woman. She used her emotions to protect her physical body from you. This doesn't necessarily mean that she doesn't like you, only that she isn't ready to be touched.

Emotional women also communicate through implication. They often don't come right out and say things, but seem to "beat around the bush." For example, if a mother wanted the emotional girl to clean her room, she would say, "Gee, I wish your room were clean!" implying the message. As well, they respond well to your implication. For example, instead of saying, "Hey honey – let's go screw," you might want to try "Honey, wouldn't it be warm and cozy if we were naked in bed right now?"

Physical people on the other hand use their bodies to protect their emotions. They tend to be very touchy-feely. They will put a hand on your arm or shoulder for emphasis. For example, a person that touches your hand as she speaks to you, both for emphasis and connection, or a woman that wants to hold your hand in public is likely to be a physical-sexual.

In communication, physical women tend to be much more direct in their communication. That is, they deal with the specific meanings of words. For example, in the room-cleaning example above, the mother would have said, "Go clean your room!" – specific and to the point. If a physical woman's mother said to her, "I wish your room were clean," our physical woman would have responded, "Well, if it is that important, be my guest – go clean it!" Physical women deal with the exact meaning of words and phrases. They don't mind hearing you tell them to "go get into bed!"

You should note here that emotional women are not necessary more feminine than physical women. In fact, if you define femininity in a very traditional sense (makeup, dresses, long hair), these are more the tendency of physical women! Emotionals on the other hand will tend to play down their looks in an attempt to draw attention away from their bodies.

Here is a chart that will outline some of the differences and preferences between physical and emotional people:

	Emotional	Physical
Main focus	Emotions	Physical body
Protects weaker modality by	Using emotions	Using physical body
Use of language	Uses inference and responds to implication	Uses and responds to directness and specifics
Concentration on appearance	Low – plays down physical appearance	High – emphasizes appearance
Dress	Tends to wear clothes that hide contours of body, light, drab, or non-flashy colors.	Tends to wear flashy, bright, form-fitting clothing, emphasizing figure.
Jewelry	Very little	Lots
Makeup	Very little if any	More, usually applied very well
Shoes	Flat, bulky or "sensible" shoes	High heels, sandals, nails painted
Cars (theirs – not yours)	Prefers "sensible," less flashy cars.	Prefers flashy, fast cars with bright colors.
Posture	Normally with toes pointed straight ahead or slightly inward, and palms and arms flat against sides or pointed slightly backwards, showing closed (protected) body.	Toes will usually point slightly outward, arms and palms slightly forward, shoulders back, head up announcing openness of body.
Gait	Walk with short steps, toes inward or straight ahead, short arm swings.	Walk with long steps, toes and palms pointed outward, long arm swings.
Enjoyment of public displays of affection (PDA)	Low	High
You deal with her on a	Mental level – talk about things that create images in her mind, about her emotions, etc.	Physical level – deal with her body and emotions (with light touches, cologne, strong sensory images)
Meaning of touch	Initially a painful or uncomfortable sensation. Becomes more acceptable as trust builds.	Strong, pleasurable feeling, connection. Helps establish closeness and trust.

To help you better understand these types, here is a list of celebrities and their sexualities (at least as usually portrayed on-screen – remember these actors sometimes play a part that may be different from their real sexuality):

Mae West	Physical
Julia Roberts	Emotional
Barbara Eden	Physical
Katherine Hepburn	Emotional
Sophia Loren	Physical
Ellen DeGeneres	Emotional
Sharon Stone	Physical
Neve Campbell	Emotional
Hillary Clinton	Physical
Annette Bening	Emotional
Monica Lewinsky	Physical

Here are some interesting points about this model:

- About 60% of all men are primarily physical-sexuals (51% or higher)
- About 60% of all women are primarily emotional-sexuals (51% or higher)
- Almost all gay men (95%+) are very high physicals.
- Almost all gay women (85%+) are very high emotionals.
  (By the way, if you determine you are a high physical male it doesn't mean that you're gay any more than if you are a high emotional woman, you're a lesbian!)
- You will usually be most attracted to women that are opposite of you. Thus, if you are 65% physical (and 45% emotional), you will often find women that are about 65% emotional (45% physical) most attractive, with all other things being equal.
- People who are right in (or very close to) the center (50% emotional, 50% physical) are known as "somnambulists" and tend to be highly suggestible. In fact, these are the people that stage hypnotists look for in their shows.
- It is neither right nor wrong to be any combination of physical and emotional. Neither one is better than the other – just different.
- A person's sexuality comes from their fathers (or a dominant male figure if the father is absent) – both women and men will tend to carry the same sexuality as their fathers (and therefore will generally be attracted to their mother's types).
- All babies start life as 100% physicals. They learn their emotionality as they grow.

So how do you use this information? First, by trying to approach the correct women in the first place. If you're in a bar and see an attractive woman, you might want to size her up first. She may have large boobs, but if she isn't your type, you probably aren't hers either. Women tend to be more adept at this matching than men are, although they aren't necessarily any more aware of this model than you.

Second, be aware of the type of language she uses, what motivates her, and how to connect with her. If she is an emotional, you shouldn't use a lot of touch. In fact, at first you shouldn't use any. Come to it slowly. Touch lightly and make sure your hands are warm! It may help to know that emotionals often view unwanted touch in the same way as pain – it may even feel physically uncomfortable. If she touches you, however, this is a very good thing! When you make love to an emotional woman, your timing is critical (at least if you want a repeat performance!). Don't go right in for the goodies. Spend lots of time on her face, lips, arms and shoulders. *Slowly* work up to her neck and chest. Touch the inside of her arms, her back, and her hips. When you finally get to her breasts and genitalia, take your time, and be gentle! Start with short attention to these areas and slowly build up. It takes her longer to get ready, so be patient.

If she is a physical, touch is a good thing, but don't overdo it. Accidental touch is the best, but some directed touch to help confirm what you are saying is also very good. Touch her on the arm, shoulder and back. As you get closer to her, stroke her hair and neck. Back and foot rubs are great. Don't be surprised if she touches you also, but don't over-interpret this. She may touch you but it isn't a sign that she's ready to sleep with you – yet! When you do sleep with this woman, you can use her physical nature to your advantage. Like the emotional woman, don't dive right between her legs! Spend lots of time exploring her body. Kiss and gently bite her lips, neck and shoulders. Run your fingers around her stomach and hips. Gently caress her thighs – first outside, then inside. Tease her by occasionally touching her breast but purposefully avoiding her nipples. When she can't stand it, take a nipple between your lips and flick it with your tongue. Your physical woman loves this kind of attention!

Applying the Models

So, how do you make use of your knowledge of these models? They work equally well in both meeting and getting to know a woman, and when you are trying to build your relationship to the next level. Let's try an example. Suppose you are interested in a woman you've just met. Size up your prospective woman into a category – try to determine how much of each type she is. Then, based on your analysis, become her "perfect" match.

For example, let's say that you've determined that she is an emotional and is auditory. You will want to deal with her on her inference level, and use auditory words. This will help you to form an immediate connection with her. Use words like "imagine" and "consider," deal with her mind, and avoid directly touching her, except by accident (this works best if it really appears to be by accident because it *implies* more!). When you speak, use auditory-based language. Remember also to keep the speed of your speech right in the middle.

Say that your woman is a physical, visual type. Here, you're going to want to slowly get closer to her, and make some slight contact with her. For example, sitting close enough for your knees to touch is a good start, or emphasizing points you make by putting your hand on her arm or shoulder. Obviously, you should stay away from her breasts, ass, thighs, and so on until she is ready for this. You'll know your physical woman is responding to you when she starts touching you back.

You should also appeal to her visual nature by using visual speech. Also, remember she is looking at you based on your appearance. Make sure you are wearing clean, neat clothes without holes in them. You should wear cologne (or use nice-smelling soap), and have your hair neatly groomed. Also, be sure to shave, unless of course, you are going for that bad-boy image.

Once you get the connection established, you can use the mirroring techniques we will discuss in the next chapter to cement the connection and begin moving her toward your goals. But, be sure to let her indicate to you when she is ready to move. Be focused and aware of her actions, and her reactions to you. If you move faster than she is ready for, she'll put the brakes on and you'll have to start all over again. On the other hand, if you don't respond to her she'll get frustrated.

To use the motivation model, you'll need to appeal to her type *at that particular moment.* Gear your communication to her in that modality. For example, if she is a socializer, tell her you want to get together for fun and to get to know her better, or plan things to do around other people. If she is an amiable, you'll want to do things that are quiet and affect her emotions such as classical or jazz concerts, or theatre. Intellectuals will want something to stimulate their minds. Poetry readings and museums are good choices here.

By the way, intellectuals and amiables will need information from you. They will consider the facts in determining if you are the person that they want to spend time with. Give them all the reasons why you are good for them (and they are good for you). Directors and socializers on the other hand are looking for action and feeling. Memories are also good. If you have a camera, be sure to bring it with you when you meet this type of woman. Capture the time you spend, and be sure to give her copies of the pictures. Let her remember the fun she has had with you.

The Art of Selling

"Wait, I thought that this book was about relationships – not selling!"

It's okay – you're in the right place. But, before we begin, you're going to have to have something in your arsenal other than a catchy line or two. In fact, these "lines" are really not very effective anyway and should be dumped. Why? First, they are too easy to counter. Second, they sound ridiculous and put you in a defensive posture, waiting for the women to respond. This is not the position we want to be in with women. We want to be in control. In fact, you're going to have to be if you want any type of long-term success.

So then, what is the "art of selling"? It *is not* convincing someone to buy something, or convincing some woman to go out with you or sleep with you. Any salesperson knows that you can't convince anyone of anything – let alone convince him or her to buy something. Besides, this is hard work! Do you want to have to work hard, or do you want to work easy? I thought so. Read on.

There are many sales techniques that work equally well in selling products and services. They also work in selling yourself. Let's look at the steps involved with these sales:

Marketing

Most people don't understand the difference between marketing and selling. Let me illustrate the difference with a story. I had a friend that used to work for a church. He wasn't a minister, so one day I asked him what exactly he did. He told me that his job was to support the pastor's work. I asked him how. He said, "Suppose that the pastor wanted to have a bonfire. It would be my job to set the date, scout a location and tell everybody where it was."

"Next," he said, "I'd have to show up early and clear the area of brush and debris. Then, I'd get a bunch of rocks and logs large enough to sit on and place them in a big circle. Then, I'd dig a pit where the fire would be. Next, I'd find the perfect tinder for the fire, clean it and place it in the pit. Then, I'd have to find the actual wood we'd use for the fire, strip the bark and put it in the pit."

"When people would start showing up, I'd have to make sure that they all had places to sit. After they were all seated, I'd get the pastor and bring him to the pit, introduce him and then I'd strike the match and hand it to him." This is what marketing is all about. It is everything you do before you actually make the sale.

In traditional sales terms, consider your own marketing strategy:

Marketing Concept	Dating Concept
Do you have a product that people want to buy?	Do you have yourself in reasonable shape for the women you want to attract, including your health, appearance, the place you live, transportation, finances, divorces, kids?
Have you studied your market?	What do you have to do to adequately sell yourself, and what type of women do you want?
Have you packaged your product?	Do you have an appropriate wardrobe, cologne, etc., to make you more appealing to your target women?
Do you know where to find your customers?	Where are the women that you want to meet?
Is your product "priced right"?	That is, have you determined what you have to offer?
Do you have a marketing plan?	Have you considered how you're going to go about meeting and dating women?
Is your product support plan in place?	Have you considered what strategy you will use in getting the women you want?
Do you have a product growth plan?	What will you do to improve your skills?

This is a pretty good list of things to consider. Let's look at each one in greater depth.

Your Product

It's time for some self-evaluation. Don't underestimate yourself and what you have to offer. Also, don't overestimate yourself – don't think that you're ready to jump right in. You're going to need some additional tools to get yourself primed and ready to sell. First, you need to be interesting and interested. If you sit at home night after night and watch television, you won't be considered top-shelf material! Get a hobby – find something that you're interested in and pursue it. In addition you will probably meet others that are interested in the same things, thus you have instant common ground and familiarity.

To be interested, all you have to do is listen. The best thing about this is, if you really listen with intent, you're probably going to learn something. You'd be surprised how interesting even the most mundane thing can be when seen through

the eyes of an enthusiast. Women are all looking for a man that will listen to them –
really listen.

When it comes to the listening department we men have it all over women.
Generally, women are talkers, not listeners. We must take advantage of this aspect
of ourselves to become a better, more attractive product to our customer. So, how
do you listen? You really can't fake this and it'll be obvious if you try. The best way
to listen is to ask specific questions about what's being said. Asking gives you two
things: first, it helps you to understand what she is talking about (giving you an
insight into her thinking and how she communicates), and second, it tells her that
you're interested. For example, if she starts telling you about her friend's problems
with her husband, you might ask her if she thinks they're well suited to be together.
If she tells you about problems at work, ask her what started them. Intelligent,
specific questions like these will give you big points!

One last issue on listening – try to avoid giving advice. Nothing is more flattering to
a woman than just being listened to. We as men are problem solvers, and usually
will try to find the answer right away. Women aren't usually as concerned with the
answers as with exploring the problem (sounds familiar you say?) If you just listen
with the intention of understanding, give yourself 100 extra points!

Your Market

Who are you going to attract? In the next chapter "The Plan," we're going to
examine this question in depth. As you begin getting yourself in order (your
"product"), you should be considering exactly what you are offering, and, more
important, who wants to buy your product. If you are well thought-out, your
market becomes obvious.

For example, if you are generally not very neat, have long hair, and are unshaven,
you are probably not going to fit in well with a woman who works on Wall Street.
On the other hand, if you are a businessman, corporately groomed, don't go
looking for a hippie-chick. Your market should reflect your product, and as we will
see, will also dictate many other aspects of your plan.

When you define your market, try to be as precise as possible. Most men make the
mistake of trying to be too broad in their market definition. They say, "I want to
meet a beautiful brunette with long legs," rather than specifying other more
important aspects of their target women. We will get into the specifics of this under
"The Plan."

Your Packaging

The way you're packaged will determine how your market responds to you. If you've decided that you want to meet a "sugar-momma" who will help you produce that play you've been writing, you'll have to look and act like the men that she is attracted to. You will want to research things that fit her mental image of these men including wardrobe, music, speech, and popular culture.

You should package yourself to fit well into your target market. One warning here: we guys have a tendency to overdo this if we're not familiar with the market we intend to approach. Remember, subtlety is the key. Less is more. If you are not part of the business community, but want to find that corporate executive, you're going to need a suit. In this case however, think conservative. Buying the latest style is probably not the best idea. A rogue color is also not going to help you much – gray, black and blue are the only business colors for men regardless of the industry.

On the other hand, if you're looking to package yourself as a rock star, you are much better off considering "grunge-chic" rather than just dirty. Women are very good at this and can spot a fake at 50 paces. Why not use this to your advantage? Ask your woman-buddy, your sister, or your friend's sister to help you pick out some clothes. Before you do this however, considering reading some of the books available on outfitting yourself. While women have a better sense of style and fashion than we do, they will often lead you down the path of a look that, while fashionable, won't get you what you want. You need to give her some guidelines and be firm about them.

I can't tell you how many times I've gone out to buy suits with a woman, only to have her bring something green or brown off the rack. "The color's so beautiful!" she'll tell me. But, going to a business meeting in a green suit says one thing to my peers: "I'm an asshole who can't dress myself!" Don't make this mistake. Get some foundation before you try to package yourself. You want to use a woman's talent in this area, but don't simply accept it Carte Blanc. Use good judgment in your packaging and keep your eye on the target.

Other important aspects to consider in your packaging are your surroundings, including your home and your car. As I've mentioned, you don't have to be rich to attract women. In fact, you don't even have to look rich, but you do have to seem somewhat planned. If she's coming over for the first time, review your place, because *she* will! She'll be looking at you and your home considering how she would look there. Don't expect that she'll miss something – she won't.

Look through your place as though you were looking through her eyes. You should get three bags and mark them, "Trash it," "Hide it," and "Wash it." Go through your home and examine everything. If it doesn't have a particular purpose for being there, put it in a bag. Here are some guidelines:

Item	Bag
Pictures of your ex-girlfriends	Hide it
"Men's" magazines	Hide it
Dirty clothes	Wash it
Old papers, books, etc.	Trash it
Other girls' numbers, addresses, love letters	Hide it
Dirty sheets/linens on the bed	Wash it
Previous marriage certificates	Burn it
Old items in your refrigerator	Trash it
Unused items in your medicine cabinet (she *will* look here!)	Hide it
Your current or last girlfriend's lingerie or "feminine things"	Hide it
Condoms	Hide it
Bondage equipment	Hide it

Also, consider the furniture. You don't have to have beautiful custom furniture, nor does it even have to match. In fact, many women will see this as their challenge – to get you "set up." Further, you're going to want to let them do this – even if you're not going to stay with them forever. It will really help you with the next woman. Even if your place has had the once-over from five different women; they will usually find something to change, especially if they're visuals (see "Communications"). Don't be offended by this – they are just trying to repackage the "love object" (you!).

But, the furniture you do have must be clean. If she won't sit on your sofa, she probably won't sleep in your bed either. Get the dog's hair off of the couch, wipe down the tables and vacuum the floors. Also, if your place has an odor, get rid of it. Women are very keen on smells, particularly bad ones.

With your car, if it isn't a late model Porsche, don't worry. Just make sure that it's clean – both inside and outside. Even an old car that looks well kept will work just fine. Also, if it isn't safe, she probably won't want to ride in it.

Where Are Your Customers?

Now that you've got your "look" in place, and you're ready to begin selling, you've got to find your buyers. Obviously, the type of customer (your market) will help you determine where you'll find them. If you're looking for a doctor, you're probably not going to find them at a rock concert, although some of the women there will be doctors.

Consider where your buyers hang out – bars, nightclubs, health clubs, even your local market are all places to find your prospects. You should also consider things like personal ads and the Internet. Like it or not, these actually work pretty well *if* you're careful about screening the women you meet. To quote a friend, "I met one women for lunch, and between meeting her on the Internet and seeing I in person a few hours later, she gained 150 pounds!"

If you are going to meet the woman of your dreams, you'll have to go through *volumes* of women. Re-read that last sentence. Obviously, you want to narrow the number of women you have to go through to find the ones that meet your target market. You will probably not get what you're looking for simply by meeting just a few women.

This is the "nailing jelly to the wall" concept – the more nails you put in, the more that is going to stick. Accept this concept now, and you'll be a success. You've got to go through many women, and in order to do this, you'll need *access* to many women. Thus, don't count out any possible venue to meet them. Consider your work, your church, your kid's soccer team, the park where you take your dog to play, classes, local organizations such as the Sierra Club, singles clubs, service or civic organizations, and so on.

Another source of meeting women are your friends that are married or already in a relationship. You can simply tell them that you're ready to meet someone new. Ask them if they have any ideas, as they'll probably know what you like. Don't be too picky, but dissuade them from trying to pre-qualify these prospects. If they give you a prospect, take it. You never know if she'll be "the one" or if she'll know "the one." Remember, volume counts here. As well, maybe this woman doesn't fit your goals, but does she fit someone you know? Why not pass her along?

Your Pricing

When I talk about pricing your product, I am referring to making yourself suitable and worthwhile for the market you are approaching. Note that, you don't have to limit yourself to one specific target – only women you meet at the opera, for example. Later, when we work on your goals, you're going to find that your target market is all around you. In fact, you're going to begin being aware of women everywhere you go. Just keep in mind that you have to have something to offer – and it doesn't have to (in fact, shouldn't) be a bank account. If you're fun, interesting, have access to a lot of friends or opportunities for excitement, you've got a great leg up.

As I mentioned before, if you don't have one or more yet, go get yourself a hobby. Your local college offers all types of classes in almost every subject. Have you ever been interested in cooking? You're going to meet a lot of women at a class like this. How about massage? This is a skill you'll never stop using. Ever wanted to scuba dive or ski? What about photography or travel? There are so many different things that you can do and all of them will help to make you more interesting as well as give you access to your market.

Another critical aspect of your pricing is your self-image. You must come to grips with your own worth. If you wouldn't buy you, then who would? Each person is special and unique in his or her own way. Obviously, if you've got some personal or health problems you need to deal with these. Get that divorce finalized and get a haircut. It's time to take inventory of just what and who you are. This subject is far too broad to be covered adequately in just a small section of this book. Again, there are many tape and book programs available to you to get your self-image in check. Get to it – your market is waiting!

Your Marketing Plan

This is the single most important part of reaching your goals. We're going to spend an entire chapter on this alone, so I won't go into it heavily here. But suffice it to say, you'll need a clear, concise plan to get you on your way and keep you going in the right direction.

Your Product Support

Product support is about servicing your customers. You'll have to make time for the women you meet. We're all busy people, but only you can decide where your schedule allows you to pursue your market. When you meet women, you'll need some time to get to know them. As you plan your day, schedule your marketing. Make time for it by setting aside specific times each week to perform the various tasks in your list. You'll find that you really don't need a great deal of time. Consider that you should probably plan to meet with at least one woman at least every one to two weeks. These can be the same one or two women, or they can be a large number, but either way, you'll need time.

You'll also need some money, but it shouldn't cost you a fortune. Remember, we're not buying women – that's call prostitution and you don't need this book for that. In a sense, you're interviewing women, finding the ones that meet your goals. An interview can take place almost anywhere and shouldn't be expensive.

Your Growth Plan

Finally, you'll need a plan to continue to improve yourself and your dating skills. As you go after different types of women, you have to "upgrade" yourself to become an even better product. One way this is done in marketing parlance is the "focus group." Women in every area of your life will act as your focus group. We'll discuss this further under "The Plan."

Prospecting

Now that we've explored some of the work of getting your marketing program together, let's look at how to prospect – that is, how to find the women you want to meet. Before you begin, you must have a specific, clear goal. The goal should be measurable and obtainable – you should walk away with a telephone number or something else just as specific. You may decide that you want to get two or more numbers. Don't settle for anything less – you deserve to have what you want.

This step involves locating the women you want to meet. Where are they found? Probably in many places, but you'll want to increase your chances of finding them by going to places where they hang out. For example, if your ideal woman is a cowgirl, then you are probably going to meet her at a country-western dance club or any place that they have line dancing. If you're looking for the business type, you'll need to go to a business district, perhaps on a Thursday or Friday, after work.

You should also consider the women you're going to approach before doing so. It also helps to know the local customs. One time, I was in a bar in Austria and tried talking to a few women but I wasn't having much success. They were polite and responded, but the conversations didn't last very long. None of these women had rings on the "married" fingers, but I just couldn't get very far. Then the bartender, being sympathetic, and obviously having had experience with men from the U.S., explained to me that women in that area wore wedding rings on the ring-finger of their *right* hands – not their left like we do!

You have to dress and act the part of the man your prospect wants to meet. Don't go to a dive bar dressed in a business suit. Likewise, don't go to a nightclub in shorts and a t-shirt. This may seem obvious, but look around. You'll be very surprised at how men dress when compared to women in the same place. If you dress correctly, you're probably going to stand out in a positive way.

In addition to prospecting via public venues, you should also consider other non-public avenues to meeting women. For example, personal ads, chat rooms and singles websites. These are great for a number of reasons; first, they offer you anonymity – particularly valuable if you are the shy type. Second, you have access to a large number of different women. Third, you can get to know them without having to actually meet them in person, and fourth, it will cost you very little if anything.

Remember, as I've mentioned before, you'll need to go through volumes of women. Don't try to meet three women and expect that you'll find the woman of your dreams unless you're very lucky! Assume that you're going to meet possibly tens or hundreds of women to find exactly what you want. The number may be far fewer than this, particularly if you create proper goals beforehand. But, it's far easier to work from the worst-case scenario than to assume nothing but successes.

The Introduction

The next step in this system is determining how you're going to actually meet the women you want to date. You need some way to approach a woman, and this really isn't as hard as most people think. However, the best advice I can give you is to drop all of the corny lines. "Hello there beautiful, what's your sign?" is a sure way to get her running for the hills (or at least to anyone else in the bar for protection).

The most important key to understand is that your level of confidence, either real or perceived, is going to be your greatest asset. If you seem confident and poised (even if you're not), you're going to be viewed as someone of worth. Much of the preparation already discussed will help you immensely here. When you know that you're packaged for success, you automatically relieve that stress. Look at all the preparation that goes into any sport. Dating is a game too – don't just jump in without getting yourself ready.

So, how are you going to approach Ms. Wonderful? You've got your confidence and poise ready to go. You go up near her and stand up straight. Take your time and be cool – rushing is perceived as nervousness. When you feel ready, say in a calm, slow voice, "Hi – nice (bar/wedding/day/whatever)" She'll respond with something like, "Yeah – nice place."

Next, pause for a moment then say, "What's your name?" She'll respond with at least her first name and sometimes her last. Remember her name! If you need to, say it a few times in your head but make sure you remember it. Here's an important fact – you'll almost always get her name. Why? Because first, it's non-threatening; second, people are conditioned to give names; and third, you've asked! Next say, "Nice to meet you."

Now, the next step is the most important – don't say another word! Your first reaction is going to be to put out your hand and give her your name. This is because of your social conditioning. Don't do this! At this point, you're trying to judge her interest. Remember that you don't know anything about her. Maybe she is seeing someone, maybe she's a lesbian, or maybe she's married. You don't know anything about her yet. Thus, you have to test the water.

What then, are you waiting for? You're waiting for her to ask you for *your* name. If she does, you've got a definite prospect and a possible sale. She is expressing some small level of interest. If she doesn't, she's either rude or not interested. This is safe and proven effective. If she asks for your name, put your hand out and tell her your name. Make sure your hands are warm and dry. If she doesn't ask for your name, just say, "Nice meeting you" and walk away. She has shown you a zero-interest level.

This introduction gets things started, but it also does so much more. You're going to learn a great deal about the woman in the first few seconds. So, make it count. You want to come off with confidence and ease, but not cocky. As you take her hand, notice her eyes. Is she saying anything in her look? Give her a slight smile and notice if it is returned. Over the next 10 minutes or so, you can carry on some light conversation, you may want to ask her to dance, but remember your real purpose is to gather information and create a connection. You want to see how her interest level grows or wanes. If she is interested, she will look you in the eye and speak directly to you. Does she touch you? Does she lean toward you? We'll cover this in greater detail in the next section, "The Pitch."

If you're not comfortable just walking up to someone and striking up a conversation (and why not?), you'll need to practice. Consider that you are just collecting information at this point. This is really the easy part. If you're not comfortable putting yourself out there, try starting simply. First, go out among people and just try to make eye contact – nothing more. You'll find that people will look back at you. Depending on what part of the world you are in, that look may last from one to five seconds, with two to three seconds being the average. This is normal and means that you've accomplished your goal.

The next step is to try to get a smile by giving one first. You may need to practice this in front of a mirror to make sure that it is natural. If your smile looks more like a smirk, you're not going to get the results you expect. Try this for a few weeks every time you're out among people.

Next, try saying "hello" or "good morning" to women as you pass them. Most will respond in kind. What you're doing here is trying to establish small successes. These successes will build to greater successes, but you have to start somewhere. Your life is not a dress rehearsal, but you do get to make mistakes. Now is the time to go perfect these skills so that you can begin using them to your benefit.

Remember, the introduction is not where you want to try to close the sale, i.e., get a phone number. You are only trying to establish contact here. Also, don't feel obligated to buy her a drink and don't make this the reason to meet her. It establishes a poor pattern up front. At one time it was considered suave to send a drink to a woman across a bar. This is very old and can put you in a bad situation. Worse yet, you may buy her the drink and have her down it and split – leaving you looking and feeling like a fool.

"The Pitch"

After you've broken the ice, you've got to deliver your message. That is, why is she going to want to get to know you? If you don't know the answer to this, how will she? By the time you begin meeting women, you should have already determined what you have to offer by performing the steps in The Plan. As well, you should have your goals worked out in advance.

Should you lie to her? Your mother would say no. I'm not your mother. It's sad but true; there are a large number of women out there that are just interested in you for what you can give them. A television show ran recently that showed 50 women all competing for the chance to marry a multi-millionaire that they had never met. It had a great audience appeal. The only thing that these women knew was that the man had money, was self-made, and was not in the computer industry! Could anything be more appalling than this? One of the women "won" and received a proposal. The other women were simply humiliated on national television, and their real agendas were exposed. Further, the real circus began after the show aired. The "winner" began to realize that she made a fool of herself, and tried to back-pedal (as did the rest of the contestants). This showed her real intentions and she was destroyed over and over again on national television.

This is a good example of a time where a lie would probably work pretty well. In fact, in this case it did! As it turned out the guy was a comedian and was just looking for attention to boost his career! Of course, he's taken more than his share of lumps, as though *he* did something wrong! If your goal is to bang as many women as possible, these types are good targets. They don't really care what you look like, where you come from or who you are. They care particularly about what you can give them and they'll go the distance to get it. So, if you are disguised as a famous producer, the ex-chairman of IBM, or Bill Gates' illegitimate brother, these women make perfect targets.

Obviously, you won't know what a woman wants until you get to know her. So, if you have a conscience, this is probably not a good approach for you as some of the women you meet will be legitimately nice people who will end up being taken in by this tack. On the other hand, if they are interested in where you live, what kind of car you drive, and what you do for a living, you may have just met your ideal mark.

Another great way to get these women into bed (make it *their* beds, by the way – you don't want them to know where you live!) is to rent a Jaguar for a night. You'd be surprised how inexpensive this can be, especially if you split the cost with a male friend who'll join you for a night of hunting. Not only will you look great but also you'll actually feel better about yourself as you're talking to women. More confidence equals greater success. If you're feeling particularly wealthy, you could even rent a room in a nice hotel to bring your woman to. In fact, you could actually get a few of your friends involved and have something of a party. These are all fun ways to attract and nail the gold digger.

On the other hand, if you are looking for something more substantial than just a night or two – ***don't lie!*** You must be absolutely honest from the start. However, don't think that you have to reveal your entire life to a woman on the first, or even the 10th meeting. As we shall see, you will want to meter out information slowly. Further, if you are doing all the talking, you're not taking advantage of nature's gift to men – talkative women!

Beyond getting a telephone number, your main goal should be to gather information. You want to come off as mysterious. You will do this by giving very little information. Instead, find out about her. With a few well-placed questions, and some sincere interest, you can keep a woman talking all night long. Keep in mind however that you want this first meeting to be brief. Ten to fifteen minutes is plenty.

This is the greatest key to being comfortable in talking with women, and in being successful in getting numbers – being a good conversationalist does not mean that you can talk. It means that you can *listen*. When you listen, don't just sit there – listen actively. That is, ask for information. It is perfectly acceptable to ask a woman general questions and let her answer them. As she answers them, you can ask her about the answers. She will continue to get more and more specific as you show interest. You will be amazed at what you can learn about a woman using this technique. Further, she will be highly flattered by this.

As you talk with a woman, don't give out everything about your life in one long sentence. You need mystery – and something to talk about on the next date. Be sparing in your delivery of information. Of course, if she asks you a specific question you may want to answer it, or you may not – that is up to you.

During this first conversation, you may want to dance, talk about the weather, whatever. But remember your main goal is to establish her interest level. There are many signs that you'll be looking for. Here are some techniques that will help you in getting and reading these signs.

Conversation and Listening

The pitch is really nothing more than good conversation. You never have to worry about making conversation with a simple technique – asking questions. Don't ask her as though you're interviewing her for a position with your company – switching from topic to topic, and don't ask her only "yes or no" questions. Ask open-ended questions that allow her to give you a detailed answer, such as, "How did you get into your line of work?" "How did you meet the bride?" or, "With such a big family, how do you keep up with them all?" The point here is to get her to start talking about herself (her favorite subject!). As she starts talking, observe her actions – you will need these observations for the next phase.

Absolutely avoid complimenting her on her looks. This is a very weak fallback position when you can't come up with something else – and women know it! Further, you're going to sound like every other man out there. Most women already assume that you like their looks (although they are very insecure about them). Saying something like, "Ohh, baby, you're so beautiful," tells her that you don't have much else to say. If you feel compelled to compliment her, find something specific and non-threatening. "Man, you've got great tits" isn't going to get you very far. Instead, try something like, "You know, the color of that blouse really brings out your eyes – it was a very good choice," or "The sound of your voice has a very soothing, melodic quality – are you a counselor?" However, you're generally better off staying away from the compliments until you've established some rapport with her; otherwise they just sound insincere.

Women like a good listener. Listening well means listening attentively and with focus. Don't let your eyes dart around the room looking for your next victim. Pay attention to her, lean forward as she speaks and watch her body language. When you ask her about things, make sure that you've been listening and direct your questions to the specifics of what she says. Don't jump from subject to subject – it shows a disinterest in what she is saying. Worse yet, it may sound like a job interview. She wants to think that you're interested in her, for her.

Mirroring

This is a wonderful technique that will bring you instant rapport with anyone. Mirroring is really just duplicating a person's movements, posture and attitude *in physiology*. I've rarely seen this mentioned in this way. What you want to do is to establish a deep, fundamental connection. It should feel natural and should come from deep within. This is why I say that effective mirroring comes from physiology, not simply copying a person's movements.

You will want to begin mirroring her after a few minutes of conversation. You need this time to get comfortable and to get the conversation going. If you start immediately, it will be obvious, and she will interpret it as though you are mocking her. After she is deep into answering her questions, slowly begin to adopt her posture. For example, if she is sitting with her left leg crossed over her right, cross your right leg over your left if you're sitting across from her. If you are sitting next to her facing the same direction, cross your left leg over your right. If her head is cocked slightly to one side, match it by tilting your head to the same side (i.e., her right, your left). Where are her hands? Are they folded neatly in her lap? Then fold yours in your lap. Is she leaning toward you? Lean toward her slightly. Try to match her posture as closely as possible.

After you've done this for a few minutes, try a test. Make a small change in your posture. For example, tilt your head to the other side, and see if she follows you, or uncross your arms and see if she uncrosses hers. It may take her a minute to change, so be patient. If she does, you've established a strong connection indicating a high interest level. This is a great sign that you are moving in the right direction. If she doesn't follow you, slowly go back to her posture, lean toward her slightly and try again in a few minutes after more communications with her in her modality (see "Communications").

You can also try mirroring her speech patterns. If she speaks softly, soften your voice. If she speaks quickly, speed up your speech – try to match her as closely as possible. By adopting her patterns, she will begin to feel very close to, and even mesmerized by you. Look deeply and directly into her eyes and see how long it takes her to blink. As her blinking rate decreases, you'll notice that she is also becoming more comfortable with you. Also, notice her breathing. It should match yours.

Evaluating Her Responses – Body Language

You want to pay particular attention to the signals she is giving you with her body. These signals tell you everything. She may use an aloof, uninterested tone with you, but if she is leaning toward you with her arms uncrossed, eyes wide open, smiling, you can probably bet that there's a strong interest. So what signs should you look for?

First, the position of her torso – is her body facing directly toward you? Is she leaning in toward you with her shoulders square? Is her back straight? These are all good signs of her being receptive to you. If she is turned away from you, shoulders drooped, or is leaning away, you'll need to do some work to get the connection going.

What about her arms? Are they crossed in front of her? This is a sign that she is uncomfortable with you and is protecting herself. Try to get her to open her arms. If she is leaning on the bar or table, note where her hands are. If they are by her face, with the palms forward, or she is playing with her hair, these are good signs. If her hands are clenched, or hidden from you, she may have something to hide (like a boyfriend?).

Check her eyes. Are her pupils dilated in a bright room? Obviously, if the room is dark, this isn't very useful, so you'll have to consider the location. Also, is she looking right at you, examining your face and looking directly into your eyes? All are very good signs. On the other hand, if she is looking around the room, or won't seem to look directly into your eyes, she is probably nervous. If this continues even after you've established some rapport, move on – she is probably hiding something.

Her skin can give you clues to her thoughts. If her skin has a color that seems to glow or flushes slightly, you are probably doing well. On the other hand, if it flushes deeply it might indicate embarrassment. Her breathing is also a good sign. As you establish connection with her, you may find that her breathing begins to match yours. She is mirroring you – a great sign!

Another great sign is touching. Does she place her hand on your arm or shoulder to emphasis a point? Does she "accidentally" brush you? These are all very good signs. You should avoid touching her directly until she has touched you. This is for two reasons. First, depending on her communication style, she may not like being touched by a stranger. Second, your touching indicates too much forward interest. As we will see, we want her to begin chasing *us*.

You will need to practice and perfect these techniques to improve your success. The best advice is to become a student of observation. Try different things to see how your target women react to you. If you're not comfortable with something, try practicing it at home in front of a mirror. Your skills will grow very quickly if you'll just use them.

Now, as the conversation progresses, you've mirrored her, and received her positive reactions, you will feel a natural cadence toward an ending. This is the time begin the next phase – the close.

Closing the Sale

Now that she's receptive to you, and you've established a bond, you've got to close the sale. I can't tell you how many times I've seen both salespeople and men looking to meet women make the same mistake – they don't ask for the sale! Now, doesn't that seem stupid? Why would you go through all of the work to begin the process only to hope she's going to jump right in and close it for you? Don't be a jerk. Get that sale!

Even if you haven't established rapport, you should still try to get her number. Why? Because it is good practice. You should get in the habit of getting numbers every time you approach any woman even if you don't plan to call her. The more you do this, the more it becomes second nature. Further, you are creating a list of backups that you'll need later.

Here's how we get her number – we ask. However, we don't ask in a wimpy, whining, pleading way. Like the rest of the pitch, we use direct and proven sales techniques. We use our confidence and posture and we ask as follows.

First, pause slightly to create some mild drama. Look her directly in the eyes with calm confidence, and then say, "What is your home phone number?" Say exactly these words and then shut up! Don't stammer, or stutter and don't look away. Keep looking right into her eyes. Again, you may need to practice this in front of a mirror.

You're going to get one of two responses. She'll either give you the digits or she'll give you one of 100 reasons why she can't. If she gives you her number, write it down on a piece of paper and put it in your pocket along with her name. Make sure it is a clean piece of paper. Don't use one that you've got three other numbers on! Also, if you're getting more than one number that night, don't let her (or others) see you do this! No woman wants to be only one in a cast of hundreds. If you have to, wait until you can get to the bathroom, and remember the number. Also, you should note some of the things she told you on that page. You will use this when you call her back.

Now, the next step is crucially important. Smile slightly and say, "It was nice to meet you" and *walk away*. Do not continue the conversation and do not wait for her response. This will seem abrupt – it's supposed to! You're actually leaving her wanting more. Also, it is a very strong, confident position and should be easy for you. Do not thank her for her time, and don't say, "I'll call you." Just leave.

What do you do if you just can't bring yourself to be this abrupt? First, get over it. You *can* do this. If you're still not comfortable with this approach and can't do it, there is another way. However, be advised that it is not as successful a technique as what I've already given you. Further, you'll really have to establish rapport and connection to be successful. Try this:

Say to her, "I've really enjoyed talking with you. You seem like a nice person and we seem to have a good rapport. Let's get together and have coffee some time and continue this conversation." Note here, you're not *asking* her if it is okay with her –

you're acting like you already know it is! You're just moving naturally to the next phase. This posture was already established when you first said hello. Note that we didn't *ask* her if we could call her. Don't give her the option to say "no" – just assume that she wants you to call her and proceed.

Now, here's a little trick that will really help you actually get her number. Before you go up to meet her, get a small piece of paper or a napkin – anything to write on. Leave one side of the paper blank. On the other side write, "Now, your real number?" When you take the pen out of your pocket (you *did* remember to bring a pen, didn't you?), hand it to her with the blank side of the paper up. Say something like, "Let me have your home phone number and I'll call you after I check my schedule."

She is either going to give you a number or she will give you excuses. If you get excuses, simply say, "It was nice to meet you," and walk away. Don't wait for her reaction – just walk. Now, go find someone else and try it again.

After she writes down her number, check to see if she's included her name. If not, write it on the page as well – remember you may get more than one number. It won't help you much if you don't know whom you're calling! If she didn't include her last name, you can ask, "What is the correct spelling of your last name?" and write that on the page as well. Pause for just a moment and examine the paper. Then, turn it over and hand it to her again. She will read the back side and laugh. This is a good way to end the conversation on a high note. Tell her it was nice to meet her, shake her hand, and leave. After you get out of sight (don't let her see you do this), note a few of the things that she told you on the paper. You will use this information later.

Remember, just because you get her number doesn't mean that you *have* to call her back. (I already hear the women groaning.) Getting someone's telephone number does not obligate you to call her. In fact, you may just be practicing here. There is nothing wrong with that, but be aware that if you don't call her back, and you happen to run into her again, you'll have to do some back-pedaling.

Follow-up

This phase involves actually setting the next meeting. It is usually best to start with something simple like coffee or a walk. If you move right in to try to set up a date, you may blow her out of the water. What you really want to do here is to continue building the connection. A short meeting is the ideal way to do this.

Your timing on the follow-up is also critical. Don't call her later that same night! Don't call her the next day, or the day after that! You've got to use time as your ally. She is going to need some time to build you up in her head. She is still high from your first meeting. If you rush to get with her before this has started to subside, she'll feel overwhelmed. Worse yet, she may think you're desperate. If this happens, you're going to have to work twice or three times as hard to counter it. It is best to not let it happen at all.

So, what is a good timeframe for calling her back? You should give her *no less* than a week, and two is better (one comedian says, "Two weeks – do you know how long that is in girl-years?"). By this time, she is coming down from having met you, but she hasn't given up on you yet either. You may want to wait 10 days or so. If you wait longer than two-and-a-half to three weeks, you've missed the opportunity. She will have forgotten about you, or will be angry that you haven't called and then you'll have to deal with that.

When you do call, make it a short conversation. Don't try to rehash all of the issues you discussed when you first met. You should ask her about something she mentioned (you noted this on the paper with her number – remember?) This tells her that you were paying attention. For example, if she mentioned that she has a cat, you might ask her how "Fluffy" is. She will be very impressed that you remembered. Then, get to the point.

When you set the appointment, have two different dates in mind. Ask her, "I wanted to get together to continue our conversation of the other evening – is Tuesday afternoon or Thursday evening of next week better for you?" As with most other aspects of these initial contacts, we are establishing posture by not begging her, and not relinquishing control. We are simply giving her a choice.

What do you do if she says that neither is good for her? Say, "I'll have to check my schedule beyond next week and call you back." **Do not** jump back in and say something stupid like, "Well, what about tonight, or next Saturday, or now…" You've got to establish some value up front, and you do this by being unavailable. Women seek value. If your time is open, it won't hold any value for her. You've got to establish that you are very busy (this is why you keep your schedule), and that, if she wants to get to know you, she's going to have to work around you.

She may come back with, "Well, what about (another day)?" Here, what you say is critical. Remember, as far as she's concerned, you're already booked until the days you've already offered her. If she gives you a day before this, explain that you are really swamped until the times you've offered, but will check your schedule. Then say, "If something opens up, I'll call you." This is an important step – remember we talked about the "backup" or standby woman? It is good to have one or more women on-call in case something else doesn't pan out!

What if she offers you a date *after* those you've already given her? Here, you can say, "That may be okay but I'll have to verify it in my calendar – I'll call you later to confirm." *Do not* simply accept the date! You've got to create value and you do this by 1) being very busy (she won't know why you're busy – could be that you're doing laundry that evening!), and 2) being in control. Never, never leave the next date or even the confirmation of an appointment up to her.

The third kind of response you can get is where she asks to confirm with you. As just mentioned, you never want to leave these things up to her – she will put you "chase" mode. Then, you'll have to track her down or worse yet, she'll leave you hanging until the last minute. So, your response to this will be, "Unfortunately, I can't leave blocks of time open. I'll tell you what – I'll call you tomorrow to confirm." Again, get that ball back in your court. You want to have control over this. She will respect you for it!

Handling Objections

All men and salespeople encounter objections. An objection isn't a "no"; it is just a request for more information. I've seen it happen so many times – someone gets a flat-out "no" and then turns it around into a "yes." As I've already mentioned, you can't convince anyone of anything. Thus, you shouldn't spend your time trying.

But, keep in mind – women are fickle creatures. So many times, they know broadly what they want, and may assume that you're not it. But, until you get the chance to make your pitch, how do you (or they) really know? If you're going to play the volume game (that is, going after many women), you will not really care when you get a "no" – it is all part of the game. You may just want to move on. However, if you want to give her another chance to win, you can handle the objection. After all, the prize is *you*!

Ultimately, there is no objection that you can't counter successfully. However, you're going to have to decide how much time and effort you want to put in to try to counter them. Countering is not the most powerful position you can take. Further, there are so many women out there I recommend that you don't put too much into any particular one, but some simple effort can be appropriate and worthwhile. If after a few minutes of countering, you're not getting anywhere – move on. Don't waste your valuable time on a loser. If she can't understand your value, then *she* is the problem – not you!

Here are some common objections and how to handle them:

Objection #1 – "I don't give out my phone number"
There may be a reason why she won't give you digits – maybe she doesn't want to give it to *you*, has a live-in boyfriend/husband at home, or maybe she's overly cautious. Be careful here and don't push too hard. Most important – don't give her *your* number and ask her to call you! That puts her back in control.

If you have a computer (you *do* have a computer – right?), ask her for her private e-mail address. Or you can ask for a cell phone number. Another possibility is to offer to call only at a specified time. If you do this, call her exactly at the time you've agreed upon. Some men ask for a pager number. I discourage this as after you've paged her, it puts her back in control to return your page. Also, don't ask for all three: her e-mail address, different numbers, and a particular time to call. Try no more than one or two other options. If this doesn't get you her number, move on.

Objection #2 – "I don't even know you"
What she is saying here is that she doesn't trust you. As well, her interest level is very low. You may need to give her more information about you to raise the interest level, but the first meeting isn't the place to do this. Your response should be quick and absolute: "You don't know me *yet*. That's why we should get together in a more comfortable setting – to get to know each other better, because I don't know *you* yet either." This will put her somewhat on the defensive.

Objection #3 – "I don't think that I'm ready for a relationship"
Say with some surprise, "Who's talking about a relationship? I'm just talking about having a drink! If that works out, then maybe we'll get to know each other better."

Objection #4 – "I don't drink coffee/alcohol"
She is playing with you, trying to see if she can make you squirm. Put it back in her lap by saying, "Oh, that's okay – how about something with a prescription?" She'll laugh and hopefully drop her pretensions. Now, you can say, "It doesn't matter where we meet as long as it's comfortable and quiet, and you can even drink water if you want."

Objection #5 – "I'm already seeing somebody"
If she says this, you should probably just move on – tell her it was nice to meet her and wish her luck with her relationship. However, if you're the gambling type you could try this. Say, "So what? Are you a fanatic or something?" She'll probably laugh. Now, you can say, "Look, I respect your relationship, but you don't seem like you're entirely satisfied with it. Otherwise, why would you be here without him? Let's meet so you can tell me what you're looking for in a man."

Even if she doesn't want to meet you, she'll appreciate your direct, ballsy attitude. Who knows? She may even be impressed enough to agree to meet you again.

Objection #6 – "I don't have time"

This is a "catch-all" objection. Everybody has the same amount of time. The question is how you use it. If something is important enough, you'll find time for it. She may be legitimately busy, but if she's interested, she'll make the time.

You can say something like, "Yes, I know about being busy. But, we really seem to have a connection, and I'd hate for us to miss a chance like this. Let's see if we can find an hour somewhere." Frankly, anyone can find an hour somewhere in their schedule. You can also make it a telephone meeting if you can't get a personal meeting. However, if she is adamant about her time, don't waste yours. Move on.

Once you've countered her objection you should go back to a posture of power and control. This puts things back on track and goes back to getting the number (if it is the first meeting), or the appointment (if you're calling her on the phone). Don't wait for her to offer – assume that she wants to meet with you; and unless she's a lunatic, she will.

The Plan

Most people put more effort into planning their vacations than they put into planning any other aspect of their life. Isn't this ridiculous? If you intend to be truly successful in your dating life, commit right now to making some plans for yourself. Start by making complete, specific decisions about what you want, when you want it, how you're going to get it and how you will know when you've found it. This chapter will help you perform this critical step.

Do not proceed until you have completed the steps in this chapter!

Most books about relationships are geared toward helping you find a permanent mate. I've already stated that I don't believe that men are monogamous and therefore don't necessarily expect that this is your goal. If it is, that's fine. If instead you just want to get laid, that's fine too. Either way, you're going to have to decide *specifically* what you want.

Maybe you want both – you want to sleep with a number of women, and then settle down with one. I personally believe that if your eventual goal is to settle down, you had better "sow your oats" beforehand. If you're 18 years old (or 20, 25, 30), and haven't been with a number of women through a number of relationships, you should re-think that whole "settling down" thing. There are so many reasons for this that they alone would fill an entire book. But, consider three of the most important points:

1) You don't have enough basis for your selection of a partner
2) You really don't know what other types of women may be right for you
3) You owe it to your partner to be skilled in relationships and the bedroom

Frankly, getting out of the relationship that you *thought* was what you wanted is going to be so much more difficult and painful than not having found it. The problem is not that there are too many divorces – there are too many marriages! Don't take this lightly! Don't use these tools to get yourself into trouble. I'm trying to help you out here!

How many women do you need to go through before you are ready to settle down (again, if that is your goal)? Obviously, only you can answer that question. Further, you can only answer that question after you have enough experience to know what constitutes enough for you. As a general guide, I don't recommend that you settle down until you are sure you have the experiences you want.

In fact, I don't recommend that you settle down until you can answer these questions affirmatively:

- Can you devote your entire personal and sexual energy to a single woman for the rest of your life? (Remember, you both may very well live to be 100 years or older!) If so, how do you know that you can?

- Can you look at your past and feel that you've had all of the experiences you could have wanted as a single person? What if you died today; would you go without missing anything?

- Do you know specifically what you are looking for in a woman? What she brings to your life and you to hers? Can you outline these items specifically, including how your life would be different with or without her?

Simply getting married because you're lonely isn't a very good idea. I believe that you're only lonely when you're by yourself and you don't like the company. In other words, getting married in this situation won't really correct the root of the problem. Work on yourself first. Then, when you're at your best and most comfortable, if you decide to marry, you're making this life-changing decision from the best place.

Let's get started on this journey. The next section will help you begin your planning.

Make Some Decisions

Men are decision makers by nature. Obviously, some are better at it than others, but we share a common ability here. You are going to get to use that natural talent to meet, woo, and win the woman (or women) of your dreams! It's time to get started making some concrete decisions for your life. Spend some time here. Don't rush to get it done. Consider the next few sections carefully – they will be part of the rest of your life!

The decisions you make here will become your goals. I want to differentiate goals from dreams here, as they are really very similar things. A dream has all of the main elements you will find in goals (I'll outline them in more detail shortly). The difference between goals and dreams is a time limit.

A time limit promotes a sense of urgency. It gives your goals real meaning and substance. It puts you on track and it gives your effort meaning. Don't make the huge mistake of doing all the work described in this book and not setting a time limit on accomplishing your goals. Worse yet, don't fail to get started!

Now it's time to get out the pencil and paper, or a word processor. You absolutely must commit your decisions to paper. The decisions you make now will affect every area of your dating life, and maybe every area of your life in general. Be careful and really think about what it is that you want. Don't cheat yourself here. Do the work up front; it will pay off, trust me!

In order to make these decisions, you must be specific and complete. If you rush this step and come up with something like, "I'm looking for a blonde with big tits," forget it. You'll have to do better than this. Besides, you deserve better. What you are creating is your road map – your plan of attack. Just as you wouldn't want to enter a battle without a plan, you shouldn't enter this battle without a plan.

Decisions About Your "Perfect" Woman

In this step you are going to "design" your perfect woman. Your personal needs and preferences will be different from anyone else's. In fact, some of the items listed below may not apply to you. That's fine, but where they apply, really think about the answers. Even if they don't apply, note that too. If something isn't really important to you, note it and explain why. Don't cheat and use words like "everything" or "anything" – the more specific you can be, the better. You will often find that your decision document will be many pages in length. If you have only a single page (or less), you didn't do your homework!

To help you answer the questions below, consider previous relationships you've had including female friends, your sister's friends, your friend's wives, and so on. Use every example you can draw from. By the way, if you're freshly out of a relationship (within a month or two), try not to rely too heavily on that relationship for your answers. They are likely to be skewed toward the woman you are missing (or away from the woman you're angry with!). Not that you should ignore it entirely however – obviously, there are many positives about this woman that you should include, or negatives to avoid! Just don't make it the main focus of your answers.

Here are the questions you want to answer:

- What does your ideal woman look like? What is her nationality, her hair and eye color, her height, her weight, her measurements, the size of her lips and her nose, and the color of her skin?
- How old is she (usually a range, like 25-35 years old)?
- Where does she come from? Is she a native of your town or is she from another city or even another country?
- What are her views on sex? Is she submissive, demure, aggressive, dominant? Is she a nymphomaniac, moderately sexed, or frigid? Are there any specialties that you want: different positions, oral or anal sex, masturbation, different locations, "risky" sex (like in the back of a car – no, not going at 90 MPH!),

bisexuality? What is her experience level? Do you want to be the teacher or the student?

- What are her political views? Is she liberal or conservative, a democrat, a republican, or a libertarian? Is she pro-choice, or pro-life? Is she pro-death penalty or not? Does she vote?

- How intelligent is she? Brilliant, well-read, smart, average, below average, or a dolt? Does she have a degree, and if so, which degree and in what area?

- Does she own a home and/or a car? Does she drive?

- Does she share your hobbies, have ones of her own or both? What kind of hobbies does she have?

- How does she dress? Does she dress in business attire, jeans and sweatshirts, lingerie, short or long skirts, sexy or conservative? Can she dress in the manner you are used to?

- Can she cook, do housework, etc.? Does she keep a neat home, is a little clutter acceptable or would she feel most comfortable with livestock? Is this skill even important to you?

- Does she have any male friends or only female friends? Does she keep in touch with old boyfriends or not?

- Is she sane, slightly crazy, neurotic, or schizophrenic? (Don't laugh – you'd be surprised how rare sanity is here in Southern California!).

- What is her level of health? Do you want someone that is very active, moderately active or a couch potato?

- What types of music does she listen to? Does she enjoy art, movies, theatre, concerts or other types of entertainment?

- Is she striving for something? Is she going somewhere or waiting for you to lead the family somewhere?

Next, go back to each question and answer this: why did you answer this way? Really think about this – it is crucial. This last question will give you more information about yourself than anything else you could ask. I'm talking about introspection here – really looking inside and seeking a better understanding. If you give this some thought, you're going to be amazed at what you find.

As you can see, there is a lot to consider here. Remember, you are defining your ideal woman. Very few of the women you actually meet will fit your model exactly (if you find one that fits exactly – make her yours!). On the other hand, you will be able to see easily if she fits closely enough to make her worthwhile. If you meet a woman that has most of the qualities you've established here, but she lacks something that you feel is critical, keep looking. I don't want you to settle – you deserve more!

Decisions About Your Goals

Now that you've decided on the type of woman you want, it's time to decide what you are going to do with her. Consider the following before you set your goals:

- How many relationships have you already had?
- What quality have your relationships been?
- Do you have enough experience to attract and keep the woman of your dreams?

Almost everyone wants to view his next relationship as the ultimate one. Frankly, this may not fit your goals. Each relationship you establish should be a springboard to the next. For this reason, don't think that you've had any failed relationships. Each one has given you another reservoir of experience to draw from. Consider what you've learned from each relationship and how it applies to the next one you're looking for. Be the man with 20 years of experience – not the one with one year of experience repeated 20 times!

Now, answer the following questions on paper:

What specifically do you need from your next relationship?
Are you looking for a one night stand, for a relationship with one or more women, or for a marriage partner?
Do you need help getting your place in order or help with your wardrobe?
Do you need to get some more experience in the bedroom?
Do you want to test out some of your new skills?
Do you need someone that will help raise your kids?

What specifically do you want from your next relationship?
Are you looking for an experience or an education?
Do you want someone that you can educate?
What kind of freedom do you want?
How will she fit into your present lifestyle, or do you want to make a lifestyle change?
Are you just looking for a friend?

What specifically do you bring to your next relationship?
Do you have any particular skills or personality traits?
Can you offer fidelity, or an exciting ride?
Can you explore deep emotions with a partner or do you want to be the "fun pal"?

Where do you see yourself in two years? In three years? In five years?
Can you picture your life in these timeframes?
What will your relationship(s) be like?

Will you have children, or will the children you already have be out of the house?
Will you buy a house, or travel the world on a boat?
Where will you live?
What about your friends?

What type of relationship do you want to have right now? In two years? In three years? In five years?
Are you looking for a friendship right now? An on-line chat buddy? Someone to go to movies with?
Do you want something more fulfilling?
Do you want one or more sex partners?
Are you looking for a long-term mate?

How do you see reaching your relationship goal?
Do you want to find your mate right now and move toward a permanent relationship?
Would you like to meet a few women and date casually to see what grows?
Do you want to just date one or more women?

As you can see from these questions, you're creating more than just relationships here. You're also designing your lifestyle. It is difficult (impossible?) to consider the types of relationships you're going to have without affecting your life in general. So much of what we do in our relationships affects our lives as a whole.

Now that you've got some idea of the relationship you want. Remember, you are crafting your ideal life. Don't be afraid to dream, but whatever you decide on – commit it to paper! In the next section, we'll put the goals you've created into a flexible, workable plan.

Set Your Plan

Did you complete the decision making process discussed in the last section? If not, *do not proceed until it is complete!* Most people go haphazardly through their life, taking only what is given to them. **This isn't good enough for you!** You deserve better! Get your decisions written down.

Consider that your life is going to change between now and when you accomplish your goals. Thus, the old adage, "Write your goals in concrete, and your plans in sand," holds true. You want your plans to be flexible enough to handle contingencies in your life. Note that I said flexible, not vague. Your goals are static – that is, they won't change much, if at all. But, your plans may change dramatically.

If we could predict the future with any reliability, setting our plans would be much easier. Obviously, we can't, but that doesn't mean that we have to leave things up to fate. In fact, we'll look at establishing very specific plans and making adjustments as we go along.

Turning Your Dreams Into Goals

Up to now, we've been working on your dreams – your dream woman, your dream relationship, your dream lifestyle. This is the time to turn your dreams into goals. Here are the specifics on what goals really are:

1) They are specific.
2) They are measurable.
3) They are concrete.
4) They reflect the picture of your life based on previous experience, a picture of the future, and your needs and wants as defined in previous steps.
5) They are exciting.
6) They have a specific timeframe for their accomplishment.

Let's examine these items.

Specific Goals
The more specific your goals, the easier they will be to reach. That may not seem right at the first, but it is! Have you never noticed that you don't seem to feel the clothes on your body, or your hair on your head unless you think about them? There is a good reason for this. Your mind actually receives upward of 60,000 pieces of data per second (some estimates place it at 200,000 and above!). That is a tremendous rate of information flowing into your brain. Obviously, much of that information isn't important to you. Further, if you had to keep track of all of that

information, you'd never be able to focus on what was really important (like not getting eaten by a tiger or punched out by some girl's boyfriend!).

A special part of your brain called the "Recticular Activating System" ("RAS") helps filter out things that aren't important to you. So, how does it determine what is important? Obviously, threats to your personal safety are pretty important. As well, things that you make important are added to this list. You may have had times in your life when something you never heard of before is mentioned, then you start hearing about it over and over again. For example, a friend starts talking about a new car that he wants to buy, and then you start seeing them all over the place. This is the function of the RAS.

When you set specific goals, this tells your RAS to tune into anything related to the goal. The more specific you get, the finer your RAS is tuned, and the more focused it becomes. Opportunities that fit with these goals seem to present themselves automatically. If your goals are vague, your RAS will not kick in to help you reach them. If they're specific, your RAS will alert you to the opportunities. So, do you want to take the easy road or the hard one? Then, program your RAS by getting specific.

Measurable Goals
One of the most important elements of any goal is the ability to know when you've reached it! By establishing measurable goals, you will always know when you're on track. If your goal is to "find a relationship," the very first woman you say "hello" to will reach your goal. After all, what is a relationship? Commit yourself to making measurable, well-defined goals.

Another important element in making goals measurable is the ability to reset them, as you get close. Some astronauts suffer from what has become known as "Moon Syndrome." Upon returning from a trip to the moon, these astronauts began suffering vague depression symptoms. It was found that these symptoms were caused by an inability to define their next goals – after all, once you've been to the moon and back, where do you go next?

Your goals will be measurable because you will want to continue to grow. By setting benchmarks for your goals you can then begin looking beyond them once you get close. This holds another advantage for you – it keeps you growing and moving ahead.

Concrete Goals
Have you ever tried to hit a moving target with a rock? How about hitting one that you can't see? Setting goals that are not absolute, or that change frequently, is a sure way to prevent you from reaching them. Your goals must be established and

complete. Otherwise you're going to spend a tremendous amount of energy trying to get…well, nowhere!

Reflect a Picture of Your Life

Most people set goals the wrong way. They say that, "Well, since last time I did (insert your last accomplishment here), this time, I'll increase that goal by 10%." You don't want to do this! After all, what is 10% based on? Why choose some arbitrary amount that isn't tied to your real needs? Your goals must represent exactly what you want, not some slight improvement on previous performance.

When setting goals you must establish the picture of what you'll look like, what you'll feel like, and what you'll be like, when you've reached that goal. You must be able to visualize yourself after you've reached the goal. After all, there must be some reason why you set the goal in the first place. If you've decided that you're going to find a specific woman and get married, you need to establish what your life will be like when that occurs. Think about how it will feel to have a companion around most of the time. Where will you live? What will your house look like? Will you have kids? The more specific you can get this feeling, the more fine-tuned your RAS will be, and the faster you'll reach your goals just as you've defined them.

Exciting goals

Face it, if what you want to accomplish isn't very interesting to you, you're not going to get moving on it. Your goals have to be big enough to be exciting. They should compel you to start. If they are boring, you'll be able to find hundreds of other, more interesting things to do.

On the other hand, don't make the mistake of setting goals that are so large they are impossible to reach. For example, you're probably not going to meet 200 women that fit with your plans in the next month. Setting this type of goal comes from a hidden desire to fail. Set large, exciting goals, but keep them in the realm of reality.

Specific Timeframe

If you don't set a timeframe for your goals and you *do* reach them, consider yourself very lucky. Frankly, you're going to have to have a reason to get to work on your goals. What are you going to do *right now* to help you reach your goals? (Finish this book, I hope!) What will you do tomorrow? What will you do next week?

If you don't do something to change things, they are going to stay exactly like they are. If you have everything you want, you're probably not going to be reading this book! Thus, what will help to light the fire under you to get started? A timeframe.

You need to set an absolute timeframe for each goal you've written. The timeframe you select should be far enough out to give you the time you need to meet the goal, but shouldn't be so far out that you never get yourself started. An example of a reasonable goal with a timeframe is to meet five new women in the next three weeks. This is soon enough to cause you some sense of urgency, but not so close as to assure that you're going to fail. Nor is it so far away that you sit around until the day it is due before getting started.

Once you set this timeframe, you need to work backward and set some interim goals. For example, if you adopt the "five women in three weeks" goal, how will you do this? You might say that the first week, you'll meet one woman at your health club. The next week, another one from the club, and one from an Internet chat room. The third week, you'll meet one from your local watering hole and another from the chat room. These are reasonable goals that are also obtainable. Simply meeting five new women may seem like a large task, but when you break it down into steps, each with their own timeframes, it isn't that big a job.

The last issue about timeframes is that they'll help make the goal exciting. As I've already said, you should be excited about obtaining your goal. If it doesn't excite you, if it doesn't add positively to your life, then why bother? Don't accept a life of mediocrity – strive for more, after all this isn't a dress rehearsal. You've only have this one chance – get moving!

Managing Your Time

So far you've been organized and methodical about setting your goals; let's continue that organization into your plan. Your plan should be an extension of your life. To begin, let's look at how your life moves from one day to another.

Each of us has 168 hours each week to do the things we do. You probably work for a living. For most people, the job takes up at least 40 hours per week. Obviously, we also need to sleep. This consumes an average of 56 hours per week at eight hours per night. You also need to eat. Assuming that you spend one hour at each meal every day, that's another 21 hours per week. You also need personal grooming time of about one hour per day. Now, if we add all this up, you got 124 hours taken out of the total 168, leaving you 44 hours per week of extra time.

Nobody I know sits around the house for 44 hours each week wondering what to do. You have things you need to accomplish each week such as gardening, fixing the roof, and seeing friends. You also need to spend some time on your hobbies (you have hobbies, right?). Let's assume that you spend the same amount of time in these areas with this additional 44 hours as you do on your job – 40 hours. This leaves you with a total of four hours each week for getting to your love life.

No matter how busy you are, there is somebody that is even busier than you. Everybody feels that they are busy. After all, what happened to those extra 44 hours of yours last week? You don't have them any more, so they must have gone somewhere. It isn't the time that's important here; it's what you do with the time you have. As pressures from outside slowly eat into our otherwise neat and tidy lives, we have to find ways to fit in some parts. For example, you may spend part of your breakfast hour reading the newspaper, or your lunch reviewing your meeting notes.

This is the way that we actually make the 168 hours each week into more. Consider this. If you're already using the 168 hours per week to do what you have to do, how are you going to find more time to get to your love life? You'll do it by making better use of the time that you already have – by fitting in the things you have to do. We call this "effective time management."

There are great books on time management that you should have on your "to-read" list. However, here are some things that will help you get a handle on this limited time. Remember, you're going to need the additional hours to accomplish your goals.

Time Management Rule #1 – Make a List

In order to be organized and get the things done that you have to, you've got to work from lists. I don't know a single successful person that doesn't do this. Here's how it works. First, put aside a small amount of time every day, usually first thing in the morning, or late the night before. You'll need about 15 minutes at first, but as you get better and more organized, this time will decrease.

Use this time to plan your day's activities. Review what was accomplished yesterday and mark it off. What you didn't get done, move to today and add it into your priority list. As you look over your day, organize each activity by its priority. "1's" are things you had better get done today, "3's" are important but can wait, and "5's" are things that can be put off until later. Note that, as time passes, a "3" priority item on your list can move to a "2" or a "1" depending on when it is due.

Throughout the day, consult your task list to see what else you have to do. If you keep going through the list, pretty soon you'll find that you have extra time left over at the end of the day. This spare time shouldn't be idle time however. If you've done this step correctly, you'll have things you can insert here or there.

One of the things on your task list should be prospecting. Based on the goals you've already established, you're going to need time every week to begin meeting women. Make sure that this is in your task list and is marked with a high priority. Your list should reflect your goals. In the example we used before, if you want to meet five new women in a three-week period, your prospecting times, callback times, and dates with the women you meet, should all be in your task list. Remember, if you don't complete a particular item on the list, like "meet two women today," then you'll need to add that item to the next day's activities.

Time Management Rule #2 – Keep a Calendar
The form of calendar you keep is important. You'll need to find a system that works well for you. It should work with and augment the systems you already have in place. If you've never used a calendar before, a simple pocket calendar with a place for appointments and a task list will do nicely. If you've used calendars for a while, review the system you're using and make sure that it meets your present and future needs.

Today, as we get more automated, many people keep their schedules on their computers. If you do this, consider that you probably only keep your business schedule on your computer at work. This makes sense in that you probably don't want prying eyes reviewing your personal life. However, you need to have your complete schedule in a single place so that you can see how things fit in. It is also a great place to review your progress toward your goals. Consider password-protecting your schedule. Most modern calendar programs allow you to create personal entries that can be password-protected. Note that some companies forbid their employees from using passwords, or securing items, or even from putting any personal information on their computers. If your firm is one of these, consider getting a system for home where you can keep the information.

"Personal Digital Assistants" or "PDA's" are becoming very popular. They offer the advantage of being able to take your schedule, your to-do list, your contact list, and so on with you when you leave the office. Many of them will "sync-up" with a computer system so that you can enter things on either the PDA or the computer and have them update each other.

Which type of calendar you select is up to you, but do invest in one. If you learn to use it regularly, you'll have found the most important secret of time management. And, you'll be able to increase those 168 hours per week into about 200 or more!

Time Management Rule #3 – Consolidate Your Activities
We all need idle time to recharge and repair. This downtime lets you slow down, but it also gives you time to accomplish important steps in your plan. For example, when you're eating a meal, you can also be reading, updating your calendar, holding a meeting, and prospecting for women. When you travel somewhere, if you ride a train – again, reading and planning are great activities. If you drive to work or to see clients, pop in a tape on a subject you need help with like time management, negotiating skills, or self-image building.

By combining two or more activities you can really increase your available time dramatically. The cell phone is the greatest tool for the single man ever invented. First, it puts you in control by making you less available. Second, you can get many of your calls done while doing something else like driving, waiting for a meeting, or shopping. If you don't already have a cell phone, consider getting one. This is also true of voice mail or answering machines. You probably already have at least one of these. Are you putting them to good use? The telephone *is not* a priority (most people think it is!). It is a tool. Let it work for you by collecting information you need, but don't let it control you or your time.

Time Management Rule #4 – Keep Non-Critical Projects as Spares to Insert When Time Permits

We all have little nagging projects that are not high priorities. These are "5's" on our task list. Obviously, they need to get done or we wouldn't have them in the first place. If you can't delegate them to someone else, you've got to do them yourself.

These are perfect projects to insert into either your consolidated or idle time. These projects generally don't require great concentration, or additional materials to complete. Further, if you have a small block of time (even half an hour), you can get many of them off your list all at once. For example, little fix-it projects around the house can usually wait until you get enough of them to fill an hour. Changing a light bulb is not a high priority, unless you'll break a toe walking through a dark room. Be sure to put these projects on your list, but wait until you can get a number of them done at once.

Time Management Rule #5 – Keep a Pen and Paper or Voice Recorder Handy at All Times

We are all creative people, and have ideas all the time. Unfortunately, ideas alone are almost worthless. Have you ever heard somebody tell you he's an "idea man" as though he comes up with valuable ideas all the time? I'll bet he's broke too! We are *all* idea men. Every one of us comes up with valuable ideas every day – even ideas that can make us rich. The problem is, we don't have the resources or knowledge to put them into action. Any idea has to be produced, marketed and supported to make any money – these are where the real talents are.

The second (and most important) reason that ideas don't usually make money is that they get lost. That is, we don't record them and they soon get forgotten. By carrying a pen and paper or voice recorder with you, you can put all of those ideas down somewhere to be reviewed later. You never know when you're going to get a flash of inspiration. Don't let these ideas slip by! You're going to need these creative ideas to help you along with your goals. Further, as discussed previously, as you program your RAS, these ideas are going to present themselves to you. You need to capture them.

One last point here on recording ideas. When an idea comes, don't evaluate it – just record it. Too many people get an idea and then begin to pick it apart, noting all the reasons why it won't work. It then just gets dropped without getting a chance. Inspiration and analytical thinking come from different places in the brain. You can't do them both at the same time (unless you've had years of practice). When you get an idea, *get it recorded!* You can review it later.

Time Management Rule #6 – Learn To Determine What Is a Priority, And What Isn't

To many people, the telephone is a priority, the laundry is a priority, and yard work is a priority. Frankly, none of these things are priorities, unless you're in the business of selling telephones, you run a drycleaner, or you do landscaping. The only time they become priorities is if they fit into your priority list. Don't put them there simply by habit.

The telephone is a great example. How many people hear the phone ring and make a dash to answer it. "Who knows – maybe my mother is sick," they say. Now, how many times in the past few months has their mother really been sick? For most of us, not very many. We spend all kinds of money on answering machines and voice mail, then we misuse this technology. You need to recognize what is and what is not a priority. You can always check the answering machine later when your open blocks of time come.

If something truly *is* a priority, you can usually hire someone else to do it. Yard work is good example of this. Usually, for $40 or less, you can have someone else come and do it for you twice a month. Consider how much time you spend doing yard work each week. Two hours, four hours, more? Now, how much time does it take you to earn $40? If it is the same as or less than the time you spend doing yard work, consider hiring someone else to do it.

The Elements of Your Plan

Next, let's look at what you're going to need to create your plan.

A Set of Goals

We've already done this (you have done this – right?) These goals will soon become our plan of action. We will start by working from each goal backward, laying out timeframes and measurements to know when we've accomplished the goal.

The Sales and Communication Techniques Previously Outlined

You should have a good understanding of the sales and communication techniques given in previous chapters. You're going to use them heavily in reaching your goals.

A Pool of Women to Draw From

Obviously, we've got to reach our prospective women. The first woman you meet is probably not going to be the woman of your dreams. She may look like it at first, but keep looking. Because the first, second, and probably third, fourth and fifth are not going to be "the one," you're going after quantity in your marketing, but quality in your sales. So, you'll need a number (possibly a large number) of women available for you to go through.

Where are you going to find your prospects? Because you've committed your goals to paper, your RAS is going to help you find these women. You'll begin to notice that they are everywhere, except your living room (unless you live in a co-ed dorm). Every time you're at a market, at church, at the post office, at the library, at a dance or health club, at work, on the Internet, with friends, on airplanes, at weddings, attending meetings, at singles events, or looking through personal ads, you'll find new women to meet.

There are three types of contacts you'll make with women. Each will need a slightly different approach. These are:

1) Work contacts
    These contacts include your work peers, employees, bosses, customers and vendors.

    The concern here is that first, you don't want to interfere with your work environment or job. Consider that if you begin dating a woman from work (particularly someone close to your workgroup), and you break up because of problems, you're going to have some tension until you, she, and your friends at work get through the breakup.

    Second, you may have problems with management. Some companies discourage relationships between all employees or between certain employees based on their work relationship ("Don't dip your pen in the company ink"). Management may also frown on relationships between employees and customers or vendors. Pay attention to these restrictions! Your job is probably worth your discretion.

    Despite these problems, I strongly recommend that you consider work-based relationships. You spend a great deal of time at work. This is one of the ways to maximize your prospecting time. You go to work every day and can get to know the women there very easily. Also, you already have something in common.

2) Personal, non-work contacts
These are women you meet in person at nightclubs, health clubs, through friends, at the store, and so on. Salespeople call these "cold contacts" because they haven't been pre-qualified yet. Thus, your first step here is to perform the qualification. We'll examine this in more detail in the next section.

3) Non-personal, non-work contacts
These include meetings through the Internet (e.g. chat rooms) and personal ads. Because of your anonymity, you have greater flexibility and some find this approach much easier. However, remember that your prospective woman also has the same distance, and can become anything that she wants to be.

By combining women from these three contact types, you are broadening your pool to draw from. The greater the selection, the more women you'll find that match your profile. Also, you'll find that you get better prospects this way, and you get a safe way to test and improve your skills in different situations.

Some plan to get to know them
You need an approach. Each of the venues just discussed provides a different opportunity for you. They also provide a different challenge. Meeting women on the Internet, for example, lets you parcel out information slowly as you feel comfortable. However, you also have to assume that the women you're talking to really are who and what they say they are. Remember the story about the 150-pound weight gain from "The Art of Selling"?

After you break the ice, you need something to talk about. I'll give you some easy to remember ways to handle this in the next section. Even though you are interviewing these women, it shouldn't seem like an interview. It is a conversation in which you'll learn what you need to know about her. This knowledge really *is* power.

Some way to "close the deal"
Just like a good novel or a sales pitch, you're going to need some elegant, directed way to end the conversation and get the number. You'll read more about this in the next section, but for now, remember this one simple key – ask! But, ask intelligently.

A set of absolutes
You'll have to define what you want and what you believe in. This is good advice for everyone. Too many people wait for a situation to occur and then ask, "Hmm, what do I really think about that?" rather than doing it the other way around. Imagine that you've defined what you believe in up front. Then, when a situation comes along, all you have to do is apply it to your yardstick. Isn't this really much easier?

For example, if you've decided that you'll give a woman no more than three legitimate dates before expecting sex, then stick to it. If you've decided that you'll only spend $40 or less on a date, don't spend $41. Are there exceptions to this rule? Well, you'll have to decide that for yourself, but I recommend that you first say "no" to any exceptions until you find at least three compelling reasons to change your mind.

Creating Your Plan of Attack

Now that we've considered what goes into the plan, let's build it. As with your goals, you'll need to commit this plan to paper. Go get a note pad and pen or sit down at your word processor right now and let's get started.

First, review your goals. If you've completed the previous steps, your goals will dictate what you need to do and by when. Let's work from your short-term goals list first.

Take your goal and work backward
Let's say your goal is to meet and marry someone within two years. First, consider your previous relationships. How many women have you dated? What was your experience? Look ahead at the date two years from now and work backward. Between now and that time, how many women are you going to have to actually date? (I hear you saying "only one – the *right* one!") Be conservative. For example, if you've dated five different women so far, you'll probably have to go through at least this number to find one that is the type of woman you are looking for. So, plan to date seven to 10 women – it is better to aim higher than to fall short.

To meet and date five women, consider your past success rate. How many women have you met in the past year to find the women you've dated? Probably at least two for one (that is, for every woman you've taken out on a date, you've probably met and talked with two), but likely more – somewhere around two to three prospects to one. Take this into consideration and do the math.

So, if you're looking to date two women in the next two years and your "hit rate" is three to one, you'll need to meet 15 women. That really isn't so bad, is it? That's fewer than eight women per year and less than one per month. If you go after one per month, you'll be well above your historic curve – and right on target. If you miss meeting one in a particular month, add that number to the next month's goals.

Plan to work within your plan
This may sound funny, but many people will go through all the work to set their goals, create their plans, and then they do something totally different. They do this because either 1) they didn't believe in the plan in the first place; 2) they don't

continue to review and adjust their plan; or 3) they allow their goals to change. Don't do this! You've already done a great deal of work so far, and now you're right at the fun part – go enjoy the success of your work!

Finally, complete your plan
Use the same system we just reviewed to create your plan for each of your goals for one year, two years, three years and so on. While you're creating this plan, include periodic, scheduled reviews of your progress. You might want to look back at your plan at least every month or two. If your plan is shorter than two years, you may need to review your plan every other week. Make your reviews fit inside the plan. You may need to make adjustments as you go along.

Put Your Plan Into Action

In order to succeed, you'll have to put the work of the last few chapters into action. If you haven't made your decisions and organized your plan, this chapter isn't going to help you very much. Go back and finish those two sections before proceeding. Don't cheat yourself – you deserve better!

Here is an important key that you'll need to get started: Not every woman will meet the goals you've laid out in your decisions. In fact, most of them won't! Thus, you'll have to find a source for a large number of prospects. Don't worry, I'll show you how to do this later in this section. For now, just be aware that you'll need to talk to a number of women.

Working Your Plan

To turn your hard work into action, you've got to get moving. For many people an exciting goal is enough motivation; others need a kick in the seat. Do something right now to get started. Don't worry about your success or failure. Go say hello to three women today, or meet at least one woman in a public setting. After all, if you don't do something today, things are going to be exactly the same tomorrow. If you don't do something to reach your goals this week, next week will be exactly the same as this one.

You'll need a place to meet the women that fit your goals.
As we talked about before, you need a set of venues to find these women. Use more than one. We talked about the three types of contacts where you meet women in the previous section. Don't count out any one before you've tried it! I know some men that would never consider meeting a woman on the Internet, or through a singles organization. Why not? How else are you going to meet women? Remember, you need volume in your marketing, but quality in your sales. Thus, every possible venue should be used to the best of your ability.

Look around at work, at your local watering hole, at the friends of your family and friends, or your service club. Consider personal ads, the local mall – everywhere. Also consider other creative venues such as cooking and design classes – obviously women will be found here and if you already enjoy these types of activities you'll have something in common. What about taking a class at your local college? If you do this, remember that you probably won't find many women in an auto maintenance class – try to be where women will be. Also, try not to be the only man in a group of women – yoga classes for example. You will stand out, but you will be viewed as "one of the gals" or gay – not the masculine image you want.

Look at your hobbies, or new hobbies that you think you'd enjoy. What about scuba diving, skiing, or sailing? If you like to read, check out a local book club or the library. On this subject, your local bookstore is another great place for meeting women. If you are looking at books of interest to you and a nice looking woman is examining the same books, you already have something in common. Why not ask her what she thinks of a particular book (suggestion: *don't* use "The Joy of Sex"!).

You'll need a way to approach these women.

There is a difference between warm and cold approaches. Warm approaches are used when you already know the woman or have some other contact such as an introduction from a friend. Here, you have something to work with. For example, if she is a co-worker, you probably already know if she is married or not, and if she may be available. You can certainly talk to her about work-related issues, and can even invite her out for drinks to discuss some aspect of work. However, *do not* ask her out for some business related purpose and then try to put the make on her! She will resent your trick and cut you off before you get started. Instead, take some time and get to know her before you ask her out. Don't be in a big hurry – use your pre-established relationship to create even more. This is a gift – don't waste it by rushing.

Cold approaches are different. Here, you don't know the woman. This doesn't need to be a barrier to meeting her, however. But you do need an organized, systematic approach. If you just run up and try to pry her number out of her, you'll never see her again. Be calm and confident. Compose yourself before approaching her and have a plan. Why not practice this on women that you know don't meet your criteria? Decide that you just want to have a pleasant conversation with a woman. You can talk about anything. Just say hello and start a conversation. This is excellent practice.

As I've already mentioned, drop the catchy one-liners. They're ridiculous and make you look foolish. If you need an opening, try this one: "Hello, My name is (your name). I saw you sitting here and just wanted to meet you." This is straightforward, elegant and has no pretense. Remember, you're not going to marry this woman – yet. You just want to see if she fits your goals. You are actually beginning the interview process.

If you must find something to use, try applying it to the situation in which you met. For example, in a store, ask her for her opinion on something you want to buy. Say, "Excuse me, do you think this color will work with my skin tone?" or "Pardon me, what do you think of this cologne from a woman's perspective?" or even "You know, I always have trouble telling which melons are ripe," (no, not the ones in her blouse!) "how do you tell?" Any of these work beautifully and will get the ball rolling. Further, they eliminate the possibility of getting shot down because your line sounded stupid.

After things are moving along you can ask her something more leading like, "Where do you and your boyfriend go for fun in town?" Obviously, you're trying to establish if she is available. As you determine that she isn't attached, try using the mirroring techniques discussed earlier under "The Art of Selling" to see if you are establishing rapport with her.

If you've spent some time talking to a woman, you can easily move the conversation to something more personal – but don't rush it! Women find men in a hurry to be a big turn-off. You might try something like, "What is your idea of a romantic date?" or "When you spend time with a man, do you prefer to go out to a show or do something more active like horseback riding?" Again, don't be too pushy – remember, you're just trying to create rapport with her. You'll move in later.

If you've spent some time getting to know her and she seems receptive, you might say something like, "You know, I was going to go to the library this afternoon, but we've had such a nice talk, I don't want to end it. Are you free for lunch so that we can continue?" If she says yes, just go with it. If not, say, "Well, I'd like to continue some other time then. Let me have your home phone number so that I can call you later for coffee." Of course, you'd better be ready by having a pen and paper available.

If you choose this approach, here are the steps you'll want to take in meeting someone cold:

1) Before you do anything else, have a simple plan in mind – don't try to wing it unless you've had a lot of experience doing this.
2) Establish her availability. Verify that she is really available and open to your approach. Check her ring finger and ask simple, non-threatening questions.
3) Establish rapport. Use mirroring techniques and conversation to create some connection with her.
4) As things get slightly closer, you can add a very subtle touch or an "accidental" brush on her arm, etc. Also, watch her for signs such as her pupils dilating, her touching your arm, or leaning toward you.
5) Get the number! If you don't ask for digits, you're not going to get them!

As we learned under "The Art of Selling," this approach, while comfortable, is really not as direct as we'd like. I suggest you use it only until you're comfortable being more direct. The direct approach offers many things that the indirect approach doesn't. First, it establishes confidence up front – something very interesting to your prospective woman. Second, it helps to protect you from "crash and burns" because you won't have to handle objections or predict what she might say. Third, it puts you fully in control.

What is the direct approach? Let's review:

1) Walk up to your prospect and make a passing comment like, "Nice store, huh?" Wait for her response.
2) Look into her eyes and ask, "What is your name?" When she tells you – *be quiet*!
3) Wait for her to ask you for *your* name, indicating interest. If she doesn't, say, "Nice to meet you and *walk away*.
4) If she does ask, she's showing at least some interest. Use the conversation and mirroring techniques to raise the interest level and create connection.
5) After you've created this connection ask, "What is your home phone number?" and wait.
6) Whether she gives it to you or gives you some excuse why she can't/won't, say, "Nice to meet you," smile and *walk away*.
7) If you got the number, go somewhere and write it down along with her name and some of the things you've learned about her.

For more specifics on this approach see "The Art of Selling."

Qualifying Your Prospect
You do this by first looking over the woman. You want to examine her for specific signs both to determine her availability and her possible receptiveness to your approach. For example:

- Does she have a ring on her ring finger? If so, you should probably just keep on looking. Some men try to believe that the ring is only to ward off potential nut cases, and maybe this is so. But, we want to improve your odds, and with so many women out there, why not just start with the bare-fingered women first?

- Is she "put together"? That is, is she dressed somewhat nicely, or is she wearing sweatpants with holes in the knees? Does she have her hair done, or up in curlers? Is she wearing any makeup? If she doesn't look like she is expecting to talk to anyone (such as in a supermarket), she isn't going to feel approachable. Many men make the mistake of thinking that this will make her more vulnerable. Instead, this almost always makes a woman feel less approachable. She'll be thinking, "How hard-up is this guy that he has to hit on me when I look this bad?"

- Does she look like she is open to being approached or just waiting for her boyfriend? It doesn't make it easier to approach a woman that is waiting for someone else. Sure, she may appreciate your company until he arrives, but you'll never get her number! You might even want to ask her this up front as an icebreaker. Say, "Hello, you look like you're waiting for someone." And then wait for her response. If she says, "Yes, my girlfriend is supposed to meet me here," you can proceed. If she say something like, "Oh yes, I'm getting engaged today!" I'd suggest that you move on.

- Don't try to approach a woman in a group of people unless you want to ask her to dance. Women in groups are difficult to get to – they use their friends to protect them. Further, she may be there to celebrate a birthday or some other event. In this case, she may not want to be bothered. Watch to see what she is doing. If she seems to be in a closed conversation with her friends, your introduction will seem like an intrusion. On the other hand, if she is looking around the room or making idle chat, you can feel pretty confident that she wants to be approached.

You'll need a way to "close the deal" – getting the phone number
Before you even approach a woman, plan to ask her for her number. Please don't go through all the work only to leave just hoping to run into her sometime later. Unless you live in a very small town, you're not going to see her again. You'll need to get her number before you say goodbye. Thus, why not have a plan?

Keep in mind that you won't know if you want this woman's number until you've talked with her for a few minutes. You're trying to find out if you really want to see her again. If, after talking to her you determine that she's not your type, dangerous, just plain crazy, or that she isn't available, don't feel obligated to take her number – unless you just want the practice. This *is* good practice by the way.

Of course, you also make her assume that you'll call her later. If you don't call her back and you run into her again, you had better have a plan to deal with her. One way to do this is to say, "Hello (remember her name?), how are you?" She'll probably give you some type of attitude. Then you can say, "You're probably mad that I didn't call you. But, I met someone that I began seeing just after we met." Now, if you want to add her back to your "working" list (probably as a "backup"), then say, "I'd like to make that up to you. What is your home phone number again?" Then, see where this takes you.

The follow-up – specifics on handling calls, setting dates, etc.
Now that you've got the number, what do you do with it? There is probably no more controversial topic among men than when you should call her back. Once you've got the number, *wait*. Don't call her back the next day, or the day after that – no matter what tickets you've already bought. You've got to hold on for a while. Don't e-mail her, fax her, stop by, or send her flowers – nothing!

Why all this waiting? No matter what you've been told, women don't want to be chased. They want to do the chasing. Have you ever tried to feed a bird or a squirrel? If you hold out your hand and walk toward them they will take off.

Instead, if you simply hold the food in your outstretched hand, they will eventually come to you. Think of women like this. Be patient and don't be pushy or in a hurry. Review the previous Follow-up section under "The Pitch" for when to call and how to set up the first date.

You'll need a "date plan"

Have a plan in your pocket that includes (possibly) multiple dates. Don't go overboard! You are interviewing her here to see if she meets your expectations. Be discriminating – after all, she will be! Your first date shouldn't be much more than coffee, lunch or drinks. You can move to other, more expensive dates if she meets your goals later.

Many men want to jump right in and start spending money like it grows in their back yards. They think that they can "spend their way into her pants." You can't unless she is a hooker. As I've mentioned before, she already knows whether she is going to sleep with you or not. Don't try to "buy" that knowledge from her. She'll probably want to prove to you that she is interested in you by bedding down!

Here are some inexpensive date examples:

1) "Quarter" date – buy a roll of quarters ($10) and go around town trying to spend every one of them. Photo booths, arcades, newspaper and magazine racks, vending machines, or rides.

2) Picnic and sunset date

3) Horse races – this is a fun and inexpensive date. You go to the track and bet on nine 2$ exactas = $18.

4) Free events like parks, museums, or fairs. By the way, avoid timeshare sales pitches!

5) Tour the city – drive around and show her your favorite sites and have her show you hers.

6) Ask her to show you what *she* thinks is a good date by planning it, executing it, and paying for it!

I strongly discourage a movie date. The reason for this is that you don't get to talk to her. Even if the movie is romantic, she's going to fall in love with the characters on the screen – not you. You're going to have to draw her in using the techniques we've discussed before. Don't waste the date watching other people have fun – do it yourself! You can go to all the movies you want with her later, after you've won your prize. Also, don't try to "cheap out" on a date. For example, don't go to an expensive restaurant and use a "two for one" coupon – very bad form. And, it will backfire on you, making you look cheap and uncouth!

At these first dates try to remember that you are interviewing her. Obviously, don't make it seem like an interview ("Well, tell me about your last two boyfriends and why you broke up."). But, let her do most (all?) of the talking. Women love to talk – and they love a man that can listen to them. Don't let her wander into all of her problems with her last boyfriend, however. That is what her friends are for. If she begins to see you as the "friend," you're never going to get to the next step. Further, breaking her of this image is next to impossible.

Expect to succeed

Now, you're going to have to get paid (no, that isn't a typo). Getting paid will be different for different men. Maybe you want to have sex; maybe you're looking for a girlfriend; maybe you want a pal to go to the movies with; maybe you need someone to help you with your wardrobe. Generally, you aren't going to know her intentions up front. She will make them known to you on her time. This is a very bad thing – *for you!* You may be ready to make your move and she'll put on the brakes. She may even couch it in something like, "I'm just not ready yet." And, she may not be. On the other hand, maybe she's just not ready for *you* – Mr. Right would have already won his prize! Further, you don't know if she'll *ever* be ready!

Thus, you're going to have to have a success plan. Decide, based on all of the things we discussed before, how you will succeed – and when you are going to move on. Further, don't share this with her! She'll just feel imposed on and put it back in your lap as though you've ruined a possibly great relationship.

Here is how this works:

1) Review your decisions about your goals from before.
   Don't forget what you've decided for yourself. Go back and review those goals regularly, at least until you have them *firmly* embedded in your mind. And even then, go back and review them periodically. This will help you to know when you're reaching your goals.

2) Determine how many times you'll *not* get to your goal before you'll move on. Establish a plan for the progress of your relationship with a woman. For example, you may decide that you expect to kiss her on the first or second date, to sleep with her on the fifth date, etc. Whatever your personal needs, make some decisions before seeing "Ms. Right." Otherwise, she will be in control!

3) Stick to it!!

Don't make exceptions to your own rules. I don't care if she is a supermodel. If things aren't progressing along your own plans – move on! Again, you won't know what she is expecting. That is part of her plan – to keep you off balance and moving along the way she wants. If she only wants you to buy her things and take her to nice places, or if she only wants you to be a willing listener so that she has someone to dump on, you're not going to know it. So, prevent it!

This seems so easy, but frankly, very few men – even with good intentions – will do it! They'll find some little honey that they just can't put down and then $10k later, they're kicking themselves for being such a jerk. Without a success plan, you're just a sitting duck!

Classifying your women

Once you've talked to a woman, you now have to decide what you want to do. Maybe you want to pursue the woman in earnest; maybe you want to run, screaming at the top of your lungs. As you meet these women, try to categorize them. You're going to find that the women you meet will fall into one of four categories:

- "1's" – These are the prime women, the ones that most closely meet your goals.
- "2's" – These are women that meet most of your goals, but that fall short in some particular way.
- "3's" – These women fail a number of your goals, but may make good friends.
- "4's" – These are women that fail most of your goals, are game-players, gold diggers, crazy, or that simply don't work well as partners. Avoid the "4's"!

Use these four categories to give you a better sense of how the women you meet fit into your plan. Spend the most time working on the "1's" and "2's," and no time on the "4's". Get to know the "2's" better and see if they can become "1's" or should be moved to the "3's" as friends, or "4's" and dropped altogether. You can use the "3's" as a good testing ground for new techniques that you learn. You may even want to spend time with the "3's" to enhance your sexual skills, pick-up skills, or dating skills. In fact, you can even ask the "3's" their opinions on your techniques and have them help you refine them.

When you classify these women, be conservative. You may meet the most beautiful woman in the world, but if she is arrogant, put her in the "3's" until she proves you wrong. Don't arbitrarily fill up your "1's" until you're absolutely sure that she belongs there. You don't want to spend all kinds of time and money on a "1" only to have her drop to a "3" or "4" later. This is a waste of your resources.

Don't forget about your "backups"

A backup is a woman that you keep on your list when your primary falls through. If you're working your plan properly, you'll probably have a number of women to draw from and will be dating more than one. Obviously, you'll have women that are "1's," "2's" and "3's" to draw from. Use your "3's" as backups. Don't use "2's" for this – these are women you'll want to move into "1's" if they can qualify.

You're not really interested in a backup as a potential partner. She may become a friend, but that isn't really her purpose here. You need to have options as you continue to pursue your goals. Women will fall through the cracks – especially as they play their games. If you have other women to do things with, it gives you real power in dealing with your "1's."

For example, let's say that "Ms. 1" is scheduled for a date with you on Friday. You show up and she pulls something on you like not being ready. "Ms. 1" is probably playing with you, or giving you "The Test." You'll have no trouble telling her, "I'm sorry – you've mistaken me for someone that will tolerate that type of behavior. Please think about that and when you've got it firmly in your mind that I won't play that game, then you can call me – but not before!" Then, you turn and walk out the door, pulling your cell phone out of your pocket to call "Ms. 3." There is nothing wrong with "Ms. 1" hearing you do this – she'll know that you have options *and* balls too!

Review Your Progress and Adjust Your Plan

Any plan that isn't reviewed and adjusted is just a list of steps. You need to review your plan for any factors that will help you reach your goals. Strive to constantly improve your skills. Read, watch, and listen to everything you can get your hands on. There are a number of publications and websites dedicated to men's issues that will be of great help in working your plan.

Every time you try something such as a new venue or a new approach, review your success or failure analytically. Why did you succeed or fail? Was it because the woman wasn't the right type, or wasn't available? Was it because you were the right type and she just had to get to know *you*? Review and continue to refine your approach.

However, don't beat yourself up for failing. Every failure is another learning experience. You're going to have to go through a number of women to get your successes. Keep at it. Some salespeople spend all of their time looking for "no's." For example, each day they keep going until they get 10 or 20 "no's" before they stop for that day. This may seem like the wrong approach at first, but keep in mind – all sales are a numbers game. They know that if they get 20 "no's" they'll also get some "yes's." Don't let the "no's" bother you. Just learn from it and adjust your approach and above all, *keep going*!

Further, you'll find that as you refine your approach, the number of "yes's" in proportion to the "no's" will grow. Pretty soon, you'll start seeing very few "no's" altogether. But, practice is the key. My father used to say that, "Practice *doesn't* make perfect – only *perfect* practice makes perfect." He was on to something. Every time you try something and it fails, you are practicing the failure. If you learn from it, adjust it and practice again. Now, you are practicing to succeed. Re-read this paragraph. Learn to practice success.

You may need to start small at first. If you're shy, you may have difficulty approaching women. Thus, try just making eye contact at first. When this seems comfortable, try smiling. Next, say "Hello." You want to build on small successes. If you're the outgoing type, but have been plagued with difficulty meeting women, try backing off somewhat. Try just saying hello and smiling. Then, analyze the responses and continue to adjust your approach.

When you meet someone new, you have no way of knowing just what condition she is in at that time. She may have just had a terrible breakup or may have been stalked! You can't predict what she has been going through before meeting you. Also, you can't correct it for her, so don't try. Just accept women where they are. They are complex, intricate people – just like you (only different!). Armed with this information, go forth and learn. Become the man that we will all consider "the example."

One great tool you can use to help review and adjust your approach is the marketing concept known as the "focus group." Here, people from the target market are brought together and asked about their responses to marketing and product issues. Your focus group includes women you've dated in the past, prospective women, your friends and family, and even the girlfriends of your friends. Why not take advantage of having these people in your life and ask them about your approach?

Note that I have excluded all of your male contacts from this focus group. Why? Because they are probably not your target market! Go to the women in your focus group and ask them what they think about your approach. Get some feedback on what they think is successful. The more examples you can get the better. Go for volume here, and ask specific questions. Don't take their criticism personally – if they have any respect for you, they are just trying to help.

Learn, adjust, test, and succeed, my brother!

Handling Your Success

If you've done the things that are recommended in this book, you will have success. However, that success can easily cause you many other problems. You're going to need a way to handle the situations that arise out of a rich, successful dating life.

This section will deal with the most common problems you will face. Obviously, there are so many more that a single chapter won't address them all. Not even in a single book! Your best advice comes from the previous chapter on "The Test." Take a strong, active role in your relationship. Be alert, and deal with problems before they become more severe. Good luck!

Problem #1 – This woman's crazy!

Yes, you are going to run into this. Most women are at least a little crazy. Some are downright lunatics! The wacky fun of this is that you're probably not going to know it up front. When you first meet Ms. Wonderful, she is going to seem very sweet, beautiful, and absolutely perfect. Only after you've gotten to know her is the psychotic behavior going to come out. She'll grow fangs, claws, and a beard. And then what do you do?

I have a rule; I ignore all neurotic statements made by normal, sane people, and *all* statements made by neurotic people. Everyone is crazy sometimes. One of my first jobs was working with people that had all types of psychological problems in a halfway house. Some had schizophrenia, some had manic depression, some were retarded, and one even killed his wife. (Maybe that one wasn't so crazy – wait, I'm just kidding!) The thing I learned early on was that crazy people don't act crazy all of the time. They seem to have "episodes" where it comes out. But, oh, when it comes out…

Whatever the reason, your woman is going to give you a big helping of the crazies at one time or another. You have a few decisions to make:

- Can you live with these bouts? For example, if she is only wacky once a month (around *that* time), can you survive it?
- Are her journeys into the nether world because of her relationship with you, or some outside problem or force? If it's not you, can you help her find a way out of the problem? If it is you, see "Problem #3 – Women's Games."
- Is she looking for someone to make the "bad guy"? If so, you don't have much choice but to move on. You really don't want to be the guy that walked in front of the target.
- Could she possibly kill you or worse – cut off your pecker? If so, *run like a bunny on the freeway!* Get out of there right now! Don't look back – just

run. If she does attack you, she will probably plead insanity; get off scot-free; garner the respect, admiration and sympathy of every other woman and talk show host out there, and you'll just be dead or dickless!

Finally, please, please don't try to save her! If she is really screwed up, you probably don't have the skills to help her. If she is already in counseling, you might consider meeting with her counselor and find out how she's progressing. You can also find out how you can best cope with the situation. If the counselor is worth his or her salt, she'll tell you straight out what you're in for. If she's in year two of a 10-year recovery program, she is addicted to crack, or some other bag of zaniness, cut your losses – there are too many other women out there.

Problem #2 – Pressure by a woman to date only her

A woman will begin this from the first moment that she starts thinking of you as the "potential boyfriend." This is something that you want to control. Don't give up this control! You may want a monogamous relationship, but make sure that it is with this woman before you commit to it.

She may try to pressure you by denying you sex, tricking you, or doing something that makes you feel insecure so that you commit against your will. Resist these tactics. You've got to remain in control here, because if you lose, you're setting yourself up for some major problems very shortly. So, how do you handle this?

If she withholds sex and you haven't had her in bed yet, it's likely that you're not going to until (and unless) you marry her. I'm not sure why anyone would want to marry someone that they haven't slept with, but many do. In a case like this, I recommend that you move on – fast! You don't want to let your "little head" commit you into something that you're not ready for!

If she withholds sex and you have been intimate with her, you've got another problem altogether. Here, she is using a "bait and switch" ploy to get you to do something that she thinks you don't want to do (and you probably don't!). In this case, tell her that you understand how she feels and will respect that. Then say, "On the other hand, I feel that sex is an important part of a healthy relationship. If you don't agree, then I'll have to find someone that does." Dramatic? Yes, but if you let this start now, you're going to be faced with it the rest of your life. This will be fine if your goal is a sexless marriage!

Another way that women do this is by dominating your time; the purpose being that if you're always with her, you can't spend time with someone else. Even if you are ready to commit to her fully, you probably don't want to spend every day and night with her, at least until you're married or have moved in together. Even if you have done these things, you should still make time for your friends. Otherwise, they'll move on without you.

If you're not ready to fully commit, you'll have to let her know that you need time away from her – for whatever reason you choose. She doesn't have to know your every move when you're not with her, and in fact, she shouldn't.

The last scenario is the "assumed commitment" where all of a sudden you realize that your fidelity is expected. Here, you and she seem to cross some invisible threshold and you realize all too late that you're committed. You must not let this happen to you; first, because you (and she) deserve better. Second, because you can't predict which one of you will cross that invisible line first (although, if it is in her best interest, it will probably be her!). Why not get it out in the open early?

You must realize that communication is the key to handling this situation. Make it clear to her that when you're ready to commit to monogamy, she'll be the first one to know it. But, until you say *specifically* that you're ready for this, she shouldn't make any assumptions. Nor should you. Just because you say you're ready for a commitment, don't assume that she is at the same time. Ask her!

As well, you can't expect her to commit to you beyond your willingness to commit to her. Remember, you can't own another person. Even if you are married, your partner can still cheat on you. You will never own anyone else, so stop trying. Just recognize that (and this goes for women too) you've got to make being together worthwhile. "Why go out for hamburger when you have steak at home?" If you're not serving steak, the lack of a committed relationship will cause one or both of you to begin looking elsewhere for it.

Problem #3 – Women's games

These games take many forms, but are almost always tests. For example, they may say that they have to check their schedule before they can commit to a date next weekend; however, you don't hear from them until Friday night. Or you've agreed to call her at a certain time and you do, but she isn't there and doesn't return your call.

Another common game is where she purposefully misquotes you. For example, you complain to her about a particular situation, like something that she did. She then expands what you said to every other situation she can come up with. Women do this almost as a rule. Their goal is to get you off balance so that the original point is lost and you're dealing with something entirely different.

Take a stand on these games. Don't accept them under any circumstance. Review "The Test" for information on handling these games and tests directly and specifically.

Problem #4 – Ex-husbands and ex-boyfriends

"Ex's" that are still in your woman's life are a nuisance at least and a territorial threat at worst. Ask yourself, "Why is he still hanging around?" If it is because they (your woman and the ex) have children together, you'll have to face this situation directly. It is better to establish a relationship with this guy from the start. He will be concerned about your influence in the lives of his children – and rightly so! For more specifics, refer to "Problem #5 – Her Children."

If the man and your woman do not have children together, you should wonder why he is still hanging around. Have they been friends for a while? If so, just what is their relationship? Is this guy hanging around in the hopes that you'll hurt her or make her mad and he'll have another shot? Is she keeping him around in case her relationship with you doesn't work out?

On the other hand, consider that if he is married, or has another relationship – maybe they really are just friends. You should never assume this however, and expect to have it proven before you accept it on her word alone. Further, what is the new wife's opinion on all of this?

Don't bother asking the woman why he's still in her life. She'll give you only one answer, "Oh, we're just friends." If you push the issue and ask if she'd ever consider getting back together with him, she'll always tell you "no." Frankly, she was with him once; under certain circumstances, she wouldn't hesitate to be with him again. And you're not going to know what those circumstances are!

You will want to determine exactly what their connection is and then handle it like any other problem – directly and quickly. If you and she have agreed on an exclusive relationship, you have an absolute right to expect that her previous relationships are over. She shouldn't invite him to join the two of you when you go out unless she's cleared that specific instance with you. Nor should you feel obligated to allow this. Some men fear appearing jealous if they don't accept another man joining them. I disagree. You have the right to build your relationship in the way you feel is appropriate. You shouldn't be burdened with another man's influence on your woman.

I don't believe in "blanket approvals" – even when the kids are involved. A blanket approval is the assumption (on the part of the woman) that her ex-husband or boyfriend is always welcome to join in events involving the kids. No way! You have the right to assume that *their* family is dissolved, and the right to create *your* relationship with her the way you choose.

You also shouldn't be bothered with running into him when you go to see her. She should have enough respect and courtesy for you to handle him outside of her relationship with you. If she doesn't give you this courtesy, I suggest that you handle it for her, or move on. Having her ex there when you arrive shows an overall lack of respect. She either doesn't care enough to have dealt with it, or she is trying to make you jealous.

As with any other game, you should bring this to her attention immediately. You can use the "When you're with me, I expect 100% of your attention" speech very effectively here. If she can't seem to keep him from coming over, she may need to get a restraining order from a court. This is extreme, but consider that you have the right to not have the ex inflicted on you or your relationship.

Problem #5 – Her children

I strongly discourage dating a woman with children that are not yours. Of course, many people do this and it is fraught with problems. Her children will always come first (as they should), and you will come second. If this changes, you've got a totally different problem on your hands – resentment/competition from the kids, problems with the ex and the family, and so on.

You will have problems finding babysitters, you will have to take the kids along with you when you go places, you'll have birthdays and holidays to remember, you'll have to deal with the ex-husband or boyfriend (see "Problem #4" above) and the grandparents. You may become financially responsible for the children. You don't have a say in how the kids act, how they are raised, how they dress, or what they do. Further, when they feel that you are taking their mother's attention away from them, you've got a battle on your hands. Despite these problems (and many others not mentioned), many men choose to date women with kids.

The first rule you must accept is that her kids will be more important to her than you. That is, they will come first. If the kids are out of the house, this isn't as big an issue as when they live with their mother. Regardless, it will be an issue sooner or later. If she decides that her love life should take precedence over her kids, you've got an even bigger problem to deal with. You'll be seen as the guy that wrecked the family.

Let's say that you do establish a relationship with the woman and her kids. You're now going to be the surrogate father. Of course, you won't have any automatic rights, such as discipline or control, but you will be likely to have all the other fun duties including having to pay for the kids' meals, clothes, braces, school supplies, or medical bills, especially if the real father isn't around.

Maybe one of your goals is to be a father. Good for you! However, do you want to make your own kids or rent someone else's? This is a big step and I strongly recommend that you speak to a professional and get it absolutely clear in your mind what you're getting yourself into. If you have even the slightest question about this step, don't do it.

Okay, so you didn't heed my warnings and you've gotten yourself involved with a pre-established family. What do you do now? Probably the most important step you can take is to establish the ground rules regarding her kids. Exactly when will they be invited to join you two and when will you have time alone? Who handles the discipline? If she handles it 100%, will she listen to your opinion? If she gets in trouble handling the kids, are you allowed to step in? If so, will she discuss this with the kids and make them comply? That is, will she stand behind you? What about spending the night? Has she discussed this with the kids? Does she have someone to watch them when she spends the night at your place?

The only possible way to handle all of this confusion is to get it out in the open early. In fact, you should have worked this out by the third or fourth date. Believe me, it doesn't handle itself. If you don't, I guarantee that you'll wind up the loser here. Remember, her kids come first!

Problem #6 – Your children

Regardless of what happens between you and a new woman, you're always going to have your children. Hopefully, you've dealt with your ex-wife and have an understanding of where and when you get to see your kids, or you have primary custody over them. Remember, you brought them into the world, and owe them everything. Further, your new woman owes them nothing.

Your new woman is not the children's mother. She may form a bond with them (and vice versa), but you will always be the father no matter what happens. Even if you stop seeing this woman, your kids will still be around. You've got to make them top priority.

My personal story illustrates this exceptionally well. My parents divorced when I was six years old. Shortly thereafter, my mother remarried and we moved over one-and-a-half hours away from my father. My mother was awarded primary custody, but my father had visitation rights every other weekend. On the day we were moving my father told me, "I get to see you every other week and I promise I will, no matter what."

For the next 10 years, every other Friday, regardless of the weather, his health, money, or whatever, he made that three-hour round trip to pick me up, brought me back to his place, entertained me all weekend and returned me on Sunday (another three-hour drive). This meant a total of six hours of drive time (and more than 300 miles) every other weekend, and *he never missed once*! Not once! In fact, he also attended my football games, school events, and holidays. Obviously, this man was committed to his kids. How about you?

This is a difficult example to live up to, but it does illustrate a point. My father didn't put his life on hold helping to raise me – he still dated. In fact, I met his girlfriends and they would often join us when we went places or did things. I enjoyed them being around, but only because I knew that my father was committed to me. He would even ask me if this or that woman could join us! I never questioned my value to my father.

I never heard any specific conversations, but I'm sure my father laid out the ground rules up front. These women used to tell me how important I was to my father and I'm sure they felt that way because they saw it. Your kids deserve their father's best as well. Your women will respect you more than you can imagine by the example you show here. My father's women did!

Decide now that you're going to discuss this with your women. You can't hide the fact that your kids are the most important to you. Decide what involvement you'll allow your woman to have in your kids' lives. Will you allow her to discipline the kids? Will you back her up on her decisions, or does she have to run them by you first? Make these (and the other numerous decisions) *before* they become an issue. You don't want to have to fight it out later.

Problem #7 – Scheduling conflicts

A relationship needs time to grow. This means that, no matter how busy you and your woman are, you'll have to make time to be together. If you don't, it will fail. Women know this intuitively. We somehow figure it out, but often after the relationship has dissolved.

If you've started dating a woman and all of a sudden, her schedule gets in the way, she's probably already gone. She has decided that she doesn't want to continue seeing you, for whatever reason. In this case, she didn't have the guts to tell you to your face. So, she just decided to be unavailable instead. You've probably figured out that I believe in confronting things head-on. It is a sign of weakness to try to hide out until something blows over. However, many women will do this trying to avoid a confrontation. I strongly suggest that you move on as well and dump this woman. If she doesn't have enough courtesy to tell you exactly what's going on, *she's* the problem – not you.

You should absolutely stop calling or writing and get yourself back to dating someone else. You'd be surprised how interested women can be when you are no longer available to them. On some occasions, (about one in four), this will cause her to start feeling that she really doesn't want to lose you. But don't wait for that. Get your calendar filled. If she does call you back, tell her you're pretty busy right now seeing other people, but if you get a free spot, you'll give her a call. Move her to a "backup" and wait for about a month. Then call her and tell her that you've finally got an open day and will agree to see her then – and only then! Keep her as a backup until she proves that her schedule is more flexible and can accommodate you.

Problem #8 – Unexpected "stop-bys"

Women do this all the time. They just stop by out of the blue to say hello. Obviously, this is rarely convenient and can make for some real zany fun! Say for example that you just brought home "Ms. Easy" and you're getting ready to make a move. Ding dong! There's the door. You go to answer it and guess who? Sure, it's "Ms. Just-Wanted-To-Say-Hello" checking in. Oh, what wacky fun you'll have explaining that your brunette "cousin" in the short skirt dropped in from the local strip club.

Even if you're not seeing that stripper, you still don't want your new squeeze just dropping by unexpectedly. What if you're innocently re-organizing your selection of "Big Butts in Bondage" videos? Could be a little messy. You'd better get a handle on this early. The best way to do this is to tell her up front that you don't accept these stop-by's. Tell her that you don't answer the door unless you know who's coming over. Explain that you appreciate it when a woman calls before coming over. That way, you can make sure you're available to give her all your attention. Women love this.

What if you just find her outside your door one early morning? Assuming that you don't have to explain away that woman wearing your dress shirt and sipping coffee, you had better make it clear that you *do not* accept people dropping in without calling first. Do not invite her in. Explain in a calm voice, "Honey, I'm very busy right now (even if you're not). I feel bad sending you away, but I can't stop what I'm doing. Please call me before you come over so that I can really pay attention to you. After all, you deserve that, don't you?" Then, agree to call her later and shut the door.

Many men feel that some women are "geographically undesirable." That is, they live too far away to make a regular relationship convenient or even possible. Certainly there are some distances that you wouldn't want to have to travel every few days. But consider this: the farther they are from your house, the less likely you'll get a "stop-by." Weekend dates (dates that last an entire weekend) can become the norm for you and her, if you both enjoy them. These are particularly good when you have started to date a woman a little more seriously, but are still looking for someone else. This way, your weekdays (and even your Friday nights) are available for the new women, and your weekend can be spent with the "distant woman."

Problem #9 – The rules change

Oh, this is a biggie! You get a relationship going really well only to have the rules change a few months (or years) into it. Have you ever heard that the best form of birth control is marriage? Before you were married, you two were banging it out every day, sometimes twice. But, once you got married, you are lucky to get it once a month.

Any element in your relationship may change. Maybe she was willing to perform some particular sex act (like oral), and refuses after the marriage starts. Or, maybe she was very conscious of her weight pre-marriage, and gains 100 pounds post-marriage. There are so many of these rule changes, I could go on for hours. However, every one of these problems has a common cause – a lack of communication. Wait – how does "the little woman" becoming "the Mack Truck" have anything to do with communication? Simple. You haven't explained your expectations beforehand.

It's sad, but true. Women often use your inability to express your needs as an excuse to do whatever they want. It has happened to me (and you) many times. We often are confused by it. But, rest assured, if you don't tell her what you want and you don't get it, it'll be your fault!

Of course, you've completed the steps outlined in "The Plan" earlier in this book, so you already know what you want. There is nothing wrong with telling her your expectations up front – and for holding her to them once she agrees. For example, if you are attracted to thin women, she needs to know that you expect her to stay that way as your relationship grows. If you prefer your women with long hair, you better tell her before she tries on that flat-top look her girlfriends are raving about. If you expect regular sex, she had better know you expect this too.

How do you handle things once the rules have changed? Obviously, you need to discuss it with her. When you do this, try not to be critical, but be direct and to the point. Simply tell her what you expect (and hopefully, what she agreed to). Then, ask her to commit to a change. Be specific and get a specific goal from her. Her first response will likely be to put it back in your lap, "Well, you said that you'd do (fill in the blank)!" Be very careful not to let her force you into something here. Tell her that you'll deal with her concerns later but right now you want to discuss yours. Don't make her compliance dependent on your doing something for her.

She may not be willing to make the change you want. Or, she may agree to it but not accomplish the goal. Men are not very good at nagging to get something done. In any case, I don't recommend this anyway. You may need to decide that you'll find another way to handle the situation. For example, if the sex has dried up, but you don't want to leave your woman, you may need to consider finding it elsewhere (see "Problem #12 – Infidelity – Yours). If she won't go out and have fun with you, you might have to get your buddies together (in fact, you should do this regularly anyway).

Finally, if all else fails, you may have to move on. You can't force someone to do something that for whatever reason they don't want to do. Always remember, your happiness and satisfaction with your life is your responsibility – no one else's. You'll have to decide what things you need to add or remove to make your life exactly what you've always wanted.

Problem #10 – Trying to spend your way into her pants

What the hell are men thinking? Society has made it "cute" for men to spend a fortune on a woman and for her to accept it – and then dump him. Is there anything more stupid? Please, please don't spend your savings on a woman. You don't need to. In fact, it rarely works.

I've had this happen many times: I get picked up for a date by a woman, she buys me dinner, or takes me somewhere fun, pays for everything and then brings me home for some good lovin'. How about you? If this doesn't happen, then you must have missed the last decade. Women are supposed to be our equals now. That is, there is nothing wrong with their paying for dates. There is something wrong if you're the only one paying and not getting anywhere with these women. You don't have to do this! Further, you don't have to spend a fortune!

If your woman expects you to pay for everything, dump her right now, especially if you're not having the absolute best sex of your life. If you're really in love with that gold digger, you'd also better seek counseling – you've got more severe problems than just being broke.

At a minimum you should expect that your women contribute to your lifestyle at least as significantly as you do to theirs. And sex is its own contribution – equally for both of you. So, don't count it here. If you take her out for dinner and a show, you have every reason to expect something back. If she isn't financially well off, she can still contribute by cooking for you or helping you to fix up your place. If the giving is one-sided, there is a real problem.

This is especially true when you consider what women really want – they want to be part of a man's life. They want to be nurturing and giving. They want to help the man they love with the skills that they bring to the table. This includes helping him with his wardrobe, his place, his friends, and so on. Many women will help you shop for gifts, wrap them perfectly and help you create the perfect note on the card. They want to help you by offering the "woman's touch." And you should let them.

On the other hand, if you're looking for a woman to do these things for you while you're out drinking night after night with your buddies, only stopping by for sex every two to three nights ("booty-call"), the problem is *you*! Both women and men deserve an equitable contribution to and from their relationships with each other. In fact, I suggest that your giving should grow with your getting. Not that you have to keep score. But, consider your buddies. You may go out one night and pay for a round of drinks. You expect your friends to return this favor for you too. Further, you know that if you're always taking, your friends will soon stop giving.

In your relationships, look for the same balance. Don't be the jerk that over-spent on the girl that dumped him. Also, don't be the jerk that squeezed the life out of some woman. Remember, your next girlfriend may be the one that just got squeezed!

So, how do you get what you want without having to break the bank? Easy – earn respect instead.

Now pay attention: you do not earn respect by spending like a Rockefeller. You get respect by being balanced and consistent; by not letting your woman walk all over you; and by expecting, allowing and telling her to do her part.

Go back and re-read that paragraph at least a few times. Get it firmly ingrained in your mind.

Many women are not that good at knowing what their contribution should be because guys think they can compete through their wallets. You may have to tell her what you want. We've all heard the stories of women saying, "He should give me whatever I ask for – after all, he's getting *me*!" Men, that type isn't worth it. There are too many women that *are* worth it. Make a career of finding only them and ignoring the others.

When you first meet a woman, you'll want to learn what *she* believes is the right balance. Thus, you don't want to tip your hand up front – don't make your first date or two a lecture on what you want her to do. Give her a few dates and see how she reacts. If she believes in the balance we've already discussed, she will begin to ask you how she can contribute. She may invite you over for a meal, or she may buy lunch. She may offer to help you pick out your next suit or may come up with tickets to a show.

Before you begin dating, decide up front what works for you. How many dates will you take her on before you expect something in return? If your answer is higher than four or five, I suggest you rethink that answer. I don't care how much you make. If you allow anything more than this, you're establishing a precedent in this relationship that you'll regret later.

This goes both ways, by the way. Don't let her force you to spend more than you want because she has a free source of tickets to the opera. By deciding up front what you'll contribute and what you expect, you're preventing this situation. Finally, *stick to it.*

Problem #11 – Falling in love before you "own" it

How many times have you gone to the electronics or hardware store to see something new that you'd already fallen in love with? You buy it and take it home with excited anticipation, only to find out that it has a fatal flaw and won't give you what you wanted. Now, by this time, you're convinced that it was the right purchase (you wouldn't have made a mistake, would you?), and you commit to making it work. After a few months of frustration, you finally relent and go back to buy the thing you should have gotten in the first place.

We've all "fallen in love" with something before we owned it. How about the time where you listened to a great sales pitch and bought something right on the spot? If you'd given it at least a day's worth of thought, you'd never have bought it. This type of impulse or emotion buying is far too common. Don't let it control your love life! Don't fall in love with someone until you've done the prerequisite homework on that person.

Does her lifestyle fit yours? Have you seen her on her good *and* bad days? Showered and unshowered? With makeup and without? When she's not on her game? Are you really ready to be a daddy to her kids? Too often we get wrapped up in the sex without considering the full ramifications of our acts. Stop and think about how your life will be with her in three months, six months, and a year. Does this vision meet your goals? If not, reconsider where you're going. You won't be able to change her to fit, just because she has those long legs and that perfect fanny. Believe me, there are just too many available women for you to try to make her into something she's not.

Remember this also – women *want* you to fall in love as quickly as possible. This gives them the control, because once you're in love (even briefly), they've got you. They control you. Thus, you owe it to yourself to ease into your relationship. Don't be available; don't be susceptible; don't be desperate. Let her come to you. Then, after having thought it over, determine if she really fits your ideal (The number "1's" we discussed under "The Plan"). If not, let her be a "2" or a "3."

Problem #12 – Infidelity – Yours

This book is not an exploration of morality. I don't presume to know your situation or motivation. And frankly, I don't care. I've already stated that I believe (and you should too), that men are not monogamous. You may have even tried to fight this fact, but that little cutie in shipping/receiving is just too much temptation for you when the wife's not around.

Most relationships work on assumptions. These assumptions become facts all to soon – especially if you don't put a stop to them. That is, the partners don't agree up front that they will be faithful. It is only assumed. If this is the case, I can absolutely guarantee that your woman will make the assumption much earlier than you. If you've taken the time to use the tools in this book, you could very well be seeing more than one woman at a time. While this will seem perfectly okay for you, your women won't feel the same way.

I'm sick to death of hearing women call men "dogs." What this really means is that women don't want to accept the way that we men are. They want us to be they way they want us to be, and we'd better conform or else! How stupid is this? Women have an equal responsibility to be the person *we* need as well – including their understanding of what and who we are. By putting their heads in the sand and just expecting us to be a certain way they are losing out. If women were happy with the way things have become in the last few decades, we wouldn't have all of the talk shows on this very subject.

Decide what you believe up front.

If you do stray (I won't use the word cheat – it may not be cheating – you'll have to consider your own situation) or have multiple partners, *do not* share that fact with the other women! You and you alone must deal with the situation. The only reason for telling someone that you were with someone else is to hurt her, make her jealous, and/or to relieve your own guilt. If you're the guilty type, don't stray. Otherwise, deal with your own guilt on your own. You may even need to seek counseling. Don't cause someone else pain because you can't deal with the situation you've created. If you're the vindictive or hurtful type, just get out of one relationship before starting the next.

Even if you don't specifically tell her, make sure that she doesn't find out! Many self-destructive men will set things up in such a way that the woman can easily discover the infidelity. If you're going to stray, you're going to have to do the work up front to ensure that she doesn't find out. Don't wimp out here! If she deserves to have you in the first place, she deserves to be protected.

Keep in mind that women have a naturally suspicious mind. They're going to assume that you're with someone else even if you're not. You've got to cover your tracks if you're dipping your pen outside your own inkwell. Come up with a story that works, and can be verified. Please don't make the mistake thinking that you can just get away with it – you can't. You'll have to cover your tracks.

You might have a very close, trusted friend that can help you out. They may be able to cover for you when you need your story verified. I've even known men that will tell their buddy's suspicious girlfriend, "Oh, he's in the bathroom right now, I'll have him call you when he gets out." Then, the guy pages his friend with a code telling him to call the girlfriend. If you're going to play it loose, you'd better make use of every tool you have available, including your friends and technology.

One last point here. There are some states that actually have laws designed to punish the man that strays, or even the other woman. Know the laws in your area before you strike out to have that afternoon rendezvous. Further, review your contracts with employers and/or clients. Many have "morality clauses" that can be applied in broad ways, including your infidelity. There are many people out there that are just waiting to take aim at anyone who doesn't perform as *they* see fit.

Problem #13 – Infidelity – Hers

Remember, you *cannot* own another person. Period. Many people think they can, but it is a ridiculous fallacy. This is often the main reason that people feel so taken when infidelity is discovered in a marriage. That doesn't mean that you shouldn't have any expectations. It is absolutely reasonable to expect that your woman will be faithful to you – *if* you've established this up front. The standard wedding vows are designed to do this. You'd better know that you're expected to adhere to these vows too.

What if you're not married? As your relationship gets more serious there will be an expectation of fidelity, especially by your woman of you. If you don't specify it up front and she *does* cheat, she's going to tell you, "We never agreed to be exclusive!" Unfortunately, she's right. So, if and when it is appropriate, tell her what you expect, and get her commitment. If she won't commit, you can bet there is a reason why – someone that she doesn't want to give up.

So, what do you do when you believe that your exclusive partner is cheating on you? First, don't just jump in and accuse her of it! She will just deny it – and then what do you do? You only have three choices here: get proof, ignore it (unwise unless you want the same freedom yourself), or approach her with your expectations.

Let's examine getting the proof first. My friend, this is by far the weakest option of the three. How are you going to do it? By stalking her? Don't do this. First, in many cases it can be illegal. Second, if she finds out about it, you're going to look like a loser. Third, you're probably going to spend a great deal of money, take a lot of time, and wind up with nothing. If she is cheating, she's going to be much better at hiding it than you. Forget this option.

If you try to ignore it and you're concerned about it, it's going to eat you alive. If she isn't that important to you in the first place, you're better off working on another woman and moving this one to your "2" or "3" category until she re-earns a place as a "1." Consider also that she may be trying to make you jealous (if you think this is the case, see "The Test" for more information).

By far, the best way to handle this situation is to approach it directly. Obviously, without proof, you can't just go up to her and say, "I know you've been cheating on me and I want it to stop!" Again, she'll just deny it. You're much better off re-affirming your expectation to be monogamous. You can say, "Honey, I just want to remind you about our agreement to be exclusive." And then shut up! She is going to say something like, "Are you accusing me of something?" To which you'll respond, "No, I'm just restating that we've both agreed to be monogamous. If that doesn't work for you, now or at any time, I expect you to tell me." Add, "Further, if you want to go out and eat hamburger when you've got steak at home, that is your business – but I would expect more from you."

The point of all of this is to get a dialog going, and to let her know that you expect her to live by her commitments. At the same time, you are telling her that you consider yourself important and worthwhile enough for her to treat you properly. If this introduction doesn't begin a dialog, but you continue to suspect her, you may need to confront her directly. If you have a suspicious nature, or have low self-esteem, this particular woman may not be your best choice. She may just be independent.

Finally, if you continue to suspect her, but do not get the proper assurances (and evidence) that she isn't cheating, cut your losses and move on. You may not own her, but you do own yourself.

Problem #14 – Women as friends

Sorry ladies – you don't really make good friends for men. Men, almost every female friend that you have ever had (or presently have) will treat you like a sexless boyfriend. If they have trouble with the plumbing, their car, or they need a ride, and their regular boyfriend is out of town, guess whom they're going to call? *You!* Further, they'll want to unload on you all of the problems that they are having.

Most likely, you keep their friendship in the hopes of getting into their pants. Some guys have female friends that they would never sleep with, but this isn't very common. If you're trying to find a way to move your relationship with her to the next level, look at Problem #15.

What if you really just want her as your friend? One of the most difficult things for guys to do is to look at a female friend the same way they view their male friends. We tend to be guarded when women are around, and are careful about what we say and how we act. This doesn't make for the kind of friendship we really want. So, what do you do?

First, make sure that the friendship is just that. As best you can, try to picture the woman just like any other male friend and treat her just the same. You shouldn't have to change your language or act differently than you would around any of your guy friends. In addition, you shouldn't be expected to act any differently by her. If one of your male friends had problems with his girlfriend, would he spend hours talking your ear off? She shouldn't either.

What about going out? You shouldn't be expected to pay for anything more than when you are with the guys. She should pay her own way; provide her own transportation, and so on. If she asks for more than this, put your foot down. Tell her how your friendships are, with both men and women, and that she isn't any different.

What if she is your friend because *she* wants more? This is a real problem. If her friendship is important to you, you'll need to deal with it at some time or another. Why not lay out the ground rules early? As soon as you feel that she is pushing for more than just being her buddy, tell her that you're not interested in her that way. Explain that if it's going to be a problem, you'll have to stop being friends.

If you wind up sleeping with her, your friendship will change. There aren't that many women out there that can handle sex with a friend and keep their friendships on the same level. If that's okay with you, forge ahead, but you'd better have an exit plan in your back pocket.

Problem #15 – Turning a female friend into a girlfriend

If you've decided that your friend would make a better lover, you're going to need to counter some of her objections right up front. Here is a little guide that should help:

She says:	You counter with:
She doesn't want to ruin your friendship	You want to use your friendship as the cornerstone of your relationship

She knows all your past girlfriends and feels uncomfortable	You are willing to put them totally aside to ensure the success of your relationship with her
She already knows everything about you	Again, this is the foundation you want to use in your relationship with her
You already know everything about her	This is why you think that you'd be perfect together
She's afraid that you'll treat her badly (like some of your other women that she's heard about)	That would never happen – we have a strong friendship and a high level of respect
She expects to go out on dates and be treated like a girlfriend	Absolutely! You will forget your past with her and start everything new – just like dating for the first time
She doesn't see you "like that" – you are more like a brother to her	She doesn't see you like that *yet*, because she hasn't tried. You need to plan a very romantic date – dinner, candlelight, and soft music, the works – to help counter this

If you're sure you want to move this friendship to something more, be persistent, but understand that you may lose the friendship instead of making her yours. If you are willing to take that risk, by all means, go for it.

Problem #16 – Losing your male friends

Guys, don't forget that if you lose your girl, you'll still have your friends – provided you don't alienate them! Your male friends are ultimately more important to you than your girlfriend or wife (just ask any married man – but do it in private if you want the *real* answer!). They will be there for you even when she isn't. They'll help you and support you when she won't. They'll understand and support you when you're not getting sex. They'll bring you up when you're down. Take care of these friendships even when you're pursuing that woman of your dreams. Someday, you'll be glad that they are there.

Remember also that your new woman is going to want more and more of your time away from your friends. This doesn't have to be a bad thing if you make quality time for your friends as well as for her. That means planning. Consider that eventually you're going to have four separate relationships going on: 1) your relationship with your woman; 2) your relationship with your friends; 3) your woman's relationship with your friends; and 4) you and your woman with your friends and their wives or girlfriends. That's a lot to consider. Each of these relationships needs their own time to grow. Thus, you should try to schedule time for each of them. Let's look at each of these separately.

Your relationship with your woman (relationship #1) is the main subject of this book. Thus, if you've followed most or all of my recommendations, you've groomed that relationship to be healthy and should feel comfortable introducing it to others. Your relationship with your friends (relationship #2) has probably been around for some time and again, and shouldn't be an issue if you've taken care of it.

I believe that you shouldn't introduce your new woman to your friends (relationship #3) immediately. In fact, I use this as a reward for my woman. Here's how this works. The first five or so dates are just between her and me. If she wants to introduce her friends to me around the third or fourth date, this is perfectly all right. In fact it is desirable, because if you make a good impression on the friends, they will help you move her to build the relationship. I introduce her to my friends only after we have established a formal relationship (with a minimal amount of the "crazies").

I do this because I don't want her getting involved with my friendships yet. Women have a wonderfully delightful way of playing male friends against each other. If you break it off with her, and she doesn't want to stop seeing you, she is liable to try to make your friends her friends too. Then, she may start pumping your friends for information; she may show up at events with your friends; she may try to pressure your friends to help her get back with you; she may start unloading how hurt she is on your friends; or she may lie to your friends about you. She may even try to get one of your friends to start dating her to make you jealous. This is just too much madcap fun for one relationship! I have seen too many great friendships completely erode because of a woman's games.

So, when you're ready to introduce your woman and your friends, you've established a basis for relationship #3 between your girlfriend and your friends. Your friends should have some time to get used to this new dynamic. They may or may not like this woman. That is their right – you don't want to force your new woman on them. They may need time to adjust to her.

Also, they shouldn't be forced to be with both you and the woman all the time – make time just for them too! You'll need this time alone with them later. So, establish this pattern up front. When they feel comfortable, they will begin recommending that relationship #4 come into play. They will suggest that you, your girlfriend, they and their wives or girlfriends go out together.

Remember this: as soon as the women meet, they're going to begin talking about you and your friends. You may have things that your friends know about you that you don't want your new woman to know – yet. Believe me, if your friends know something about you, so do their girlfriends. And you just can't keep these women from talking to one another. Further, it doesn't even seem to matter if the girls like each other! Just why do you suppose that they always go to the bathroom in pairs? It *isn't* so that one of them can guard the door while the other uses the facilities!

What about competition between your friends and your girlfriend? I have seen many women that feel threatened by their man's friends. This is a real problem that you're going to have to handle up front. If you don't, your woman is going to handle it for you – by cutting your friends off! You can't imagine the lengths some women will go through to prevent you from seeing your friends. I've actually had women erase telephone messages or send back letters and gifts. You don't want this. It will have two very bad effects – first, you will lose your friends, probably permanently; second, your friends will think you're "pussy-whipped" and you'll lose their respect.

What then, can you do to handle this? First, you've got to make it clear that your friendships are important to you and you will not allow them to dissolve. Period. Second, you've got to help your girlfriend understand that your friendships aren't threatening to her. Explain that you absolutely will need time alone with your friends. She will have to accept this as part of your relationship with her. Recommend that she use this time to maintain her own friendships. This is especially important in the beginning of any new relationship, as you want to establish good habits up front. It is much more difficult to try to introduce them later after a bad pattern has been created.

Problem #17 – She hits, kicks, bites, or otherwise attacks you

As I've mentioned before, there is absolutely no reason for violence either by you or against you. No exceptions. The more calm you remain when things get heated, the more animated she is likely to become, trying to get you to react. This can easily escalate into violence by weak people.

Frankly, it isn't likely that she is going to do any real damage to you unless she comes after you with a knife, tries to hit you with a car, or throws something heavy at you (all of these have happened to me!). However, the problem here is highly insidious. If she smacks you and you hit her back – even in self-defense –*you* will be seen as the guilty party ("Men don't hit women…"). Welcome to one of the many double standards you get to face every day. Very few people will believe that *she* would try to hurt *you!*

There is one and only one way to deal with this situation. Call the police, have her arrested and press charges – every time. Do not hesitate; do not give her another chance. Violence is not cute, nor is it acceptable behavior in any circumstance. She should never tolerate being hit, nor should you. Expressing one's emotions through physical violence in any manner is a sign of mental illness. We've already dealt with the craziness issue earlier. You are probably not qualified to counsel her on proper behavior, nor should you try – leave it to the professionals.

It is important here to differentiate consensual and non-consensual behaviors. If one of you likes a little spanking once in awhile, wants to be tied down during sex, or even has more extreme sexual fantasies. This is a very different thing from outright battery. How do you know what is acceptable and what is not? Simple – just ask yourself, "Is this a consensual act between two adults?"

Sadomasochism ("SM") is defined as "the erotic and consensual exchange of power," and covers a lot of ground when it comes to relationships. SM practices include the infliction of pain and also the taking or giving of control to another person. As well, many other fetishes are included in under this heading.

Sadomasochistic behavior is present in many relationships and is not considered the deviant sexual practice that it once was. In fact, if you've ever held your girlfriend's hands down on the bed while you made love, by some definitions, you've practiced SM. The obvious difference here between abuse and SM is *consent*.

I bring this up here because of the general confusion of what is acceptable and what is not. The keys to the difference if you're not sure are the issues of eroticism and consensuality. Many women have "rape fantasies." That is, they may have secret fantasies of being overpowered by a man in a sexual way, but they would never want to be raped. Criminal rape is an act of violence and lacks consensuality. SM is a consensual exchange of power, and includes the erotic element. By the way, statutory rape is criminal rape between an adult and a child. This is because children are not considered capable of giving appropriate consent.

Problem #18 – You're in a relationship with her and she tells you that she just wants to be "friends"

I have some female friends, but I wouldn't want to sleep with them. You probably do too. If you have friends that you do want to sleep with, ask yourself – are you friends with this woman in the hopes of getting close enough to bed her? If you're honest, this is probably the case.

The fact is, in most cases, women don't make good friends for men. Why? First, they tend to become something of a "sexless girlfriend." That is, they will ask you to take them places, fix their car, and so on, all without sex. Second, if you're trying to bed this woman, you're going to have problems. She probably only sees you as a friend. Third, you'll have to put up with all the inherent craziness she has just as if she were your girlfriend. This is true whether she has a boyfriend (you'll get all the dirt of how this guy is mistreating her) or not (you'll get all the dating problems and personal problems). If you *do* decide to move on this, please review "Problem #15 – Turning a female friend into a girlfriend" for more information.

If you've been dating her and she tells you that she wants to be "just friends," you're probably not going to counter this one easily. First, you have to tell her, "You know, I have plenty of friends. That isn't what I'm looking for between us." She'll then do one of two things. Either she'll give you the ultimatum, "If we can't be friends, we just can't see each other any more," in which case, you're better off dumping her. Or, she'll not want to lose you and will agree to keep the current relationship.

At this point, you'll need to find out what she thinks the problem is. That is, why she wants to turn your relationship into a friendship. Is it because she wants to see someone else? Is it because she doesn't feel like she is getting what she wants from you? When you finally find out why she feels like she does, either try to counter it (better done through action than words), or simply accept it if you're not willing to become the person she wants, and break it off.

Problem #19 – Breaking up

As you date women, there will be times that you have to break up. Perhaps because she doesn't fit your goals, she's a nut case, or because you've found someone that you really want to be with exclusively. For whatever reason you feel you need to break up with her, do it directly and quickly. But also do it wisely; don't just flare up or react.

Okay, so this is easier said than done. Often breakups are due to some ongoing tension or fight. Then, when it hits the fan, one of you blows up and ends it. You usually know when things are beginning to fall apart. If you know or think that the breakup is pending, try to get yourself prepared. Here are some things to consider:

1) Do you have any of your personal things at her place? You want to get those back as soon as you can *before* the breakup. Otherwise, they will be used for bargaining, for spite or "held hostage." For example, she may say, "Well, if you want your things, you'll have to buy me that bracelet you've been promising me all this time." Or, she may want to keep your things until you give hers back (reasonable).

Let's look at another situation. You and she may have special photos or videos that you wouldn't want to share at family reunions. Letters and gifts may be part of these too. You can absolutely bet that she is going to want them destroyed when you break up. What you do with these is up to you. But if they are at her place, you must remember that they are there and decide what you're going to do about them.

2) Does she have things of hers at your place? Women are notoriously good at this. They will leave little harmless things at your place both to mark their territory and to have a reason to contact you after a breakup. Keep in mind that they may not necessarily want to get back together with you; they may just want to yell at you some more!

3) Don't break up with her on holidays, birthdays, or anniversaries. Not only is this callous and insensitive on your part (and boy, will her friends hear about it!), but it may forever taint that day for her, especially if she is in love with you.

4) Get your locks changed if you think there is even the most remote possibility of her having a key. Even if she gives you back the key, *get the locks changed!* The key she gives you back isn't the only one she has – trust me!

5) Don't get your friends (or her friends) involved in the breakup. Do it yourself, by yourself.

When you've decided that you are going to break it off, get to it. Here are some guidelines to help you:

1) Do it as soon as you decide to; don't wait until some "good" time. That time never comes.

2) Do it cleanly and all at once. You wouldn't cut a dog's tail off piece by piece – you'd do it all at once and get it over with. The same holds true for breaking up. Don't try to "let her down easy."

3) Be considerate of her feelings, but don't back down. Don't waiver, and don't tell her that maybe you can get together again later. This is unfair to her.

4) Don't promise to keep in touch, unless you plan to stick to it. Usually this is just a lie to make *you* feel better.

5) Don't promise to do anything for her. Some men do this as a way to "buy" themselves out of the relationship. Just make it a clean break.

6) Don't give her false hopes. Don't tell her that maybe, after you "get your head together" you can get back together.

7) Don't unload all of the reasons why you don't love her any more. Be concise and to the point – all without emotion.

8) Don't burn your bridges. You may decide that you want to see this woman again in the future after all. If you do, don't berate or humiliate her. Be direct and considerate.

9) Don't promise to be her friend unless you really mean it. See Problem #14 for more information.

After you break it off with her, give her some time to heal. She will probably start calling you the very next day, "just to talk." You shouldn't take these calls or call her back. She'll have to come to grips with the breakup. If the two of you have mutual friends together, ask them not to shuttle information between you and her. Explain that you're just trying to do what's best for her and that their attempts to help reduce the hurt for you both is appreciated, but it is also misdirected.

Depending on how scorned or vindictive she feels, you may be in for a battle. She may try to use your friends, your family, your work, even the courts against you. You'll have to hunker down and take the blows until she finally gets tired of it all or she meets someone new.

Problem #20 – She Wants "To Talk"

Ohhh, this doesn't sound good! Every man I know is terrified by the sentence, "Honey, I want to talk about our relationship." Why? Because it means that they are going to hear about all the things that they have done wrong. I've never heard of any woman saying this, and then telling her man how great he has been in their relationship, or how supportive he's being. Of course, the women reading this right now are thinking to themselves, "Well, if men only *were* supportive, then maybe we wouldn't have to tell them off all the time!"

Further, it is almost always going to happen when you're at your most vulnerable. For example, you're exhausted, in bed and just starting to fall asleep; you are getting ready to go to work and today you've got that big meeting you've been worrying about all week; or you come home from work and just need a couple of hours of down-time to recuperate. You know that you're vulnerable. Your woman knows you're vulnerable, and she knows that you know that she knows! Then, why do they do it?

Like many other aspects of the relationship, women are compelled to do these things. There seems to be something about the way they're wired. They just can't help themselves. Also, all the training they've received all of their lives in how to handle you tells them that this is perfectly acceptable and that you should rise to the occasion. Unfortunately for you, it is almost always couched as "just an innocent question." If you get mad and take her to task for it, she'll just say, "Hey, I'm just asking – why do you have to be such an ogre all the time?" Now, you've got another battle on your hands in addition to the first one. It will just escalate from here.

Men, when you get this from your woman (and you *will* get it), you had better make a quick decision. If you've got the energy and if you've prepared yourself in advance, you may decide to move ahead and respond to her right then. However, I strongly recommend that you put her off instead. As I've already mentioned, you know that you're not in the best place to deal with this question – that is by her design. So, why try to deal with her on her level?

You should tell her, "Honey, you've asked a valid question. But, I'm not able to give it the attention it deserves right now. Why don't we plan to discuss it (at some future time)?" Make sure that the date and time you pick is really a good one – she's going to hold you to it. Also, please don't make the mistake of giving her any old answer just to pacify her. You'll only be in worse trouble when that time comes and you're not prepared.

So, how do you prepare for this? Give it some real thought. You're going to get this someday, so why not prepare for it from the beginning? Consider how you've contributed to your relationship with her. *Do not* try to use something like, "Hey, remember that great sex we had last week?" She'll just counter with "Gee, I didn't think it was so good!" Oh, that hurts!

Instead, remember the times you've been supportive, and try to include things you've said or done that have been particularly caring or nurturing toward her. If she's important enough to you, you should be trying to do small and considerate things regularly. Don't try to do a few big things to catch up. Women don't think that way. They are more concerned with quantity of these gestures than size. One big gesture is still just a single gesture. Many small gestures weigh much more heavily. Just be sure to note these things in your mind because you'll need them soon. She may not remember the loving things you've done for her, but she'll absolutely remember every time she's been hurt or disappointed. Further, you'll have enough trouble remembering them yourself!

Also, don't try to use the gifts you've given her. That isn't what she's asking about. Women put a lot more weight on the things we do that affect them emotionally, much more so than we do. She may appreciate the earrings you gave her, but not as much as that note you left on her nightstand. These little romantic things go a long way. You should consider reading some of the great books out there on romance written for men. Unless we make it a priority, we just don't think of these things as often as women (and sometimes not at all!).

After you've created this mental list, there is nothing wrong with writing it down. In fact, here's a great tool to help you handle this situation. Write down the things you can remember you've done that have been supportive, caring, and loving, and put it in your pocket. When you sit down with your woman at the agreed-upon time, wait for her to tell you what a lout you have been. Then say, "Honey, I spent some time thinking about this," (she won't believe you), "and I put together a list of some of the things that were special to me." Then, pull out the list and give it to her.

First, she's going to be floored that you took some time to actually think about your relationship with her (points!), and even wrote it down (big points!). Second, they will help *her* remember what you've done to support your relationship. This is a good time to ask her what *she's* done. Of course, she'll already have her mental list ready to go (women do this!) At least now you've turned a potentially explosive situation into a sparkler. Next, she is probably going to give you a (much defused) list of things that she wants to you start doing. Don't just "yes ma'am" her. Keep referring to your list. Say, "But honey, I *do* that – see?" Also, listen to her – she may be telling you exactly what you need to know to save your relationship somewhere down the road.

Women tend to keep everything you do on a scorecard. If you hurt them, it goes on the scorecard. If you miss a romantic opportunity, it goes on the scorecard. If they ask you for something and you don't do it, add it to the scorecard. Unfortunately, they usually don't add the good things you do to the scorecard – it's not that kind of scorecard! What your woman is really saying is that she wants more of the emotional content in her relationship with you. By now, you should have already handled the "change him to fit my ideal" problem (see "The Test"), but women still expect us to live up their idea of romance.

Don't let her force you into doing something you don't want. Don't agree to take her on some expensive, romantic cruise just to placate her. Further, don't let this be a bargaining session. Too many men will try to buy their way out of this situation rather than dealing with it head-on. You've got to take a stand and help her to remember that you're the guy she fell in love with, not the reason for her dissatisfaction with her life. Also, don't be the guy that acts as her showpiece for her friends. Just because her best friend's lover did something, doesn't mean that she can expect you to do it too.

Pass It On!

Men, we have a responsibility to our brothers, our sons and our friends to get the message out. We need to pool our successful experiences and continue to grow and evolve just as our society needs to grow and evolve. A man's role a century or more ago was much more specific and identifiable. Today these roles are less well defined, and we are expected to be many different people all at once.

In order to be successful in our roles we need a better way of communicating. Traditionally, we have been expected to learn all of our roles from our mistakes. However, with these ever-expanding roles, this task is no longer the simple clumsy act it once was. We are now expected to succeed in our relationships with others almost immediately. In fact, even small failures can lead to all sorts of trauma, embarrassment, humiliation, removal from society, and even legal problems. And these expectations are growing.

Women are expecting more from us too. In our defense, our capacity to meet these expectations is also expanding, but the rate is falling behind the demand. Why aren't we pushing for a more efficient way to give men the tools that they need to be successful in our relationships *before* they are needed?

As I've mentioned in this book, women receive relationship training from many sources. We are limited almost exclusively to a few publications, our male friends, and our experiences. If we have rich and varied experiences, great – but if these experiences lack, our relationships with women tend to suffer.

Thus, I implore you, pass what you've learned on to others. Continue to improve your skills, learn, experiment and then share. This is very difficult for men as we are not good at discussing our relationships. We tend to see this as un-masculine. Certainly, we have an ingrained understanding of much of our world and discussing it seems trite. When it comes to our relationships on the other hand, it is often too difficult. If society is to grow beyond the problems men face over and over again with women, we need to become the catalyst for its growth, or get out of the way.

We are in a state of change right now. Where that change will take us depends on who takes the leadership role. Moreover, it seems that everyone has an agenda and wants to be the driver. Religious leaders, government officials, media personalities, and artists are all claiming to have the answer to organizing and promoting this change. Perhaps they do to some degree. However, I believe that the change must start from the individual. Expecting larger organizations to effect this change is a sure course for disaster.

But, don't these organizations of individuals represent a larger body of thought? They do, but it is by all measure "popular thought." I've already spoken out against the mainstream view, as it tends to promote status quo rather than real evolution. Further, all organizations exist first for their own survival. Nothing is more difficult than disbanding any organization. They try to survive against enormous odds and when they find they don't fit anymore, rather than just ceasing, they make small, painful changes. It's like trying to whip a U-turn with the Queen Mary!

Thus, we are obligated to work together to improve the lives of everyone in our community. Both men and women want better relationships and better lives. We deserve fulfillment and satisfaction. But, it starts with us individually. Why not buy copies of this book for your friends as gifts? You know that birthdays, Christmas, and other holidays are coming up – why not be prepared?

By working together with a common goal, we can make a difference. The new century is a fresh canvas waiting for your stroke of color.

Welcome to the beginning.